WALKING

RANDY A. MYERS

Trust In Jesus!

Randy A. Myers

CONTACT AT:

Randy A. Myers
Founder & CEO of
International C.O.P.S. Ministries
P.O. Box 892
Clinton, TN 37717-0892
www.copsministry.org
copsministries2003@yahoo.com

WALKING IN OBEDIENCE
Published by CreateSpace Independent Publishing
© 2013 by Randy Myers and CreateSpace Independent
Publishing

International Standard Book Number:
978-1492202974

Unless otherwise noted, all Scripture quotations are taken
from the Holman Christian Standard Bible®, Copyright ©
1999, 2000, 2002, 2003, 2009 by Holman Bible Publishers.

"He Will Carry You" Written by Scott Wesley Brown
copyright ©1982 Birdwing Music/BMG Songs, Inc

DEDICATION

I want to dedicate this book to my family, Lisa, Daniel, Sarah and Rebekah.

To Lisa: I love you more than life itself. You have stayed with me through all of the good and the bad and especially when you didn't understand me. You have loved me in spite of my failures. You are a true gift of God and I cannot tell you enough how much I love you!

To Daniel, Sarah and Rebekah: You know the hardships that we have been through as a family but more importantly you know and understand that without Jesus in our lives we would have not made it.

Keep walking in obedience and surrendering to Jesus. Keep living for Him knowing that nothing else matters in our life. Without Him we are nothing.

I don't know where I would be today if it were not for Jesus. I also do know where I would be if it were not for you all being in my life today.

I am so very proud of all three of you. Keep living for Him regardless of your failures and keep being in total surrender to His will. One day you will hear, "Well done thou good and faithful servant."

CONTENTS

WALKING IN OBEDIENCE

Preface

I want this book to be an encouragement to every person.

We've heard all our lives the stories of those in the Bible about how people were obedient to the voice of God and we have often thought, "Wow that was awesome." Some people even think, "Man, I wish I could do something like that, or I wish God would use me in some way like that to help people."

The beauty of that is God CAN use us. He WANTS to use us. All it takes is for us to walk in obedience to the Holy Spirit and yield ourselves to HIM on a daily basis. Spend time with Him in prayer and reading the Bible and create a relationship with Him.

Your obedience to God is the very key that unlocks the portals of heaven that allows Him to pour out His blessings!

My good friend and Associate Pastor, Ed Washington, told us something one day that by God's grace I will never forget. He said there's a simple explanation of being HOLY:

"Having Our Lives Yielded"

In order for us to walk in obedience, all we need to do is yield our hearts and minds to Jesus Christ daily and watch HIM work and move not only in our lives, but in the lives around us.

Lead on O King Eternal

FOREWORD BY
Kristi Neace

What does it mean to *walk in obedience*? According to the *Free Online Dictionary* the definition of obedience is a "Compliance with someone's wishes or orders or acknowledgment of their authority; submission to a law or rule."

As parents we desire obedience from our children. Police officers seek obedience from those they are instructing, and likewise, God looks for obedience in our daily relationship with Him. The Bible tells us in 2 John 6, *"And this is love; that we walk in obedience to his commands. As you have heard from the beginning, his command is that you walk in love."* If we love God, then we will be obedient to Him. We will allow ourselves to become exposed and vulnerable to *His* will and *His* purposes for our life, because His ways are higher than our ways and His knowledge exceedingly infinite. Obedience is listening and responding to God's promptings, even when it doesn't make sense in our own finite minds.

Woven within the stories of this book, I believe you will discover a life wholly surrendered to the will of God. Randy has shared his own personal stories which display moments of human reasoning versus belief in a God who neither knows no bounds nor is hindered by constraints of time, space or reason. Has he ever questioned the Holy Spirit's promptings? Sure. Did he wonder about his own sanity at times? I'd have to venture that he did. Yet, the pattern of his life reveals a heart steadfast in a steady

Savior. And, he has encountered God in very real, yet out-of-the-ordinary ways, something most Christians desire, but never experience.

Without further ado, I encourage you to read every story with an open heart. Ask God to reveal what is holding you back from walking in obedience and experiencing the same or even greater power. Allow yourself to be transformed into a usable vessel in which He may demonstrate His redeeming power. Let us remember the words of Jesus spoken to His disciples, *"Truly, truly, I say to you, he who believes in Me, the works that I do, he will do also; and greater works than these he will do; because I go to the Father."* John 14:12

Kristi Neace, Founder of Badge of Hope Ministries

Chapter 1   **The Beginning**

Many times over I felt I was supposed to write a book. As a police officer there are so many things I could write about, some funny things, some not so funny.

And when my son wrote his first book, *I Heard God's Voice*, I felt as if God was saying, "Get it done!"

There are many things I could write about and many places I could start. There have been so many miracles in my life that I don't even know if I could remember them all. I could talk about how at the age of fourteen God spared me one winter day from being killed or losing a leg while I was "jumping" or "hopping" a train while it was moving. I was late for school and needed to cross the railroad tracks to get on my way. As I grabbed the rail of the train and began running with the train, I pulled myself up on the ladder when all of sudden my foot slipped through the ladder rail and landed onto the wheel of the train. Thank

God the wheel had a metal cover over it that kept me from being pulled under the train and being run over by the metal wheels and cut into pieces.

I could talk about how God spared me the time I fell asleep at the wheel of my car while driving through Kentucky on I-64 when I was on my way to college in Chattanooga, TN. I ended up in the median after missing several cars and doing a "360" in the median. A man pulled over and checked on me and asked if I was ok. Thankfully I was and did not hit anyone.

But I choose to start with the miracle of the day, when I met my wife, Lisa Dawn Combs, in Kanawha City, WV. What an amazing and beautiful lady she was and is. I met her in the spring of 1986. The night I met her, before I even knew her name, I remember telling my friends, John W, John G, and Kevin W, "Guys, that's the girl I'm going to marry right there." In fact, Lisa and I were married in September of 1986.

Some of our family members and some of our friends told us we would never make it. But 27 years later we're still together!

During the first few years of our marriage, we talked about having kids but Lisa's doctors were telling her that she could not have any children. They followed it up by saying, "Well, even if you do get pregnant you won't carry full term because you're too small."

Unfortunately, their words came to pass in 1989 when Lisa had a miscarriage and we lost our first child, Victoria Brooke. To this day, I think of her and wonder what she would be like. Going through the loss of a child was difficult and I wouldn't wish that on my worst enemy. Had my wife not given her life to Jesus in the summer of 1988, I believe things would have been a little different in terms of how she handled the crisis.

At this time in our life, Lisa and I attended the Maranatha Outreach Center in Belle, WV with Pastor Terry H. Pastor Terry is a great man of God and helped us greatly through this trial in our life but just a few months later, we got a new pastor. We loved Pastor Terry so much and we didn't want him to go, but he explained to us how God was leading and assured us that we would love this new pastor.

In October of 1989, we met our new pastor who ended up being one of the most beloved friends of our lives and we would become very close with over the next several years.

In November 1989, we had pastor and his wife over for dinner one night. While eating dinner, a conversation took place about how Lisa was brought up to believe that women do not speak in church or even pray if there was a man present. I remember pastor saying, "That explains it." We looked at him and asked for clarification because we did not understand what he was talking about. He stated, "Many times I wanted to ask you to pray either over the offering or to close us out of the service, but every time the Holy Spirit would check me and not let me do it." He stated, "One time I was so bound and determined to call on you and ask you to pray but I felt like the Holy Spirit shook me and said, 'You will NOT ask her to pray.'" He said, "Now I understand why." I was amazed at his story but more importantly, I knew this pastor was a man of God.

On December 24, 1989, I remember being in a church service. God was moving in a great way. A member of the church (Jane B) had lost her mother and her brother within two months of each other and was going through an understandably difficult time. This lady stood and asked for prayer to help get her through this difficult time.

I leaned over and whispered to my wife, "Honey, would you go stand by her for support?" My wife declined and said, "No".

Immediately, pastor spoke up and said, "Lisa, I know how you said you were taught about praying in church with men present, but I believe the Holy Spirit wants you to pray for Jane. Would you please come and pray for her?"

Without hesitation my wife said, "Yes" and walked up and stood beside Jane. I have to be honest and say, I was shocked. I couldn't believe it. But there was my wife standing up in front of the church with people looking at her. Not only did she pray for Jane, but before she prayed she testified for the first time in her life! I have no idea what she said today but I remember her obedience not just to the pastor of the church but to the Holy Spirit in her heart. After Lisa testified she then prayed. When she said, "Amen" there wasn't a dry eye in the church.

What happened next has changed our lives forever!

After Lisa prayed, a man, Ben S, came walking up carrying his daughter from the back of the church and said, "Pastor, it is on my heart that Elizabeth pray for Lisa. Would that be ok?" Elizabeth was a beautiful little girl with blonde hair and was only three years old. She was in her daddy's arms. Pastor gave the microphone to Ben so his daughter Elizabeth could pray for Lisa. At the age of three years old, I remember this little girl asking Jesus to heal my wife and allow her to conceive a child. Two months later Lisa conceived and in November of 1990, our son, Daniel was born! HALLELUJAH!!!!

What a miracle!!! What an amazing thing! But the story is just beginning.

During labor Daniel went into distress. Something was blocking the birth canal and Daniel's heart rate went up to 210 beats per minute. The nurses came in and rushed Lisa down the hall into the operating room and told me to come with them.

The next thing I knew, I was in scrubs and standing beside my wife who was laying on the gurney with all of her insides looking at me. Jokingly I looked at Lisa and said, "Well, honey, I guess I can say now that I know you inside and out."

After the doctor got Daniel out of Lisa's belly he discovered what the problem was..... Lisa had a tumor the size of a grapefruit. The doctor had to perform a partial hysterectomy on my wife. They later told her that she wasn't supposed to have any children at all, so to be thankful for the one. Getting pregnant again on only one tube and one ovary probably would not happen.

I'm really thankful for doctors and I know they are used of God many times to heal people, but I must tell you they are not the ultimate authority in medicine. I'm thankful that this time they were wrong.

Seventeen months after Daniel was born, Sarah was born in April of 1992, and she looks exactly like her beautiful mother.

During Lisa's pregnancy with Sarah, Lisa and I encountered another hard situation. During the third trimester, Lisa said she had not felt Sarah move in about five days and was concerned. Lisa and I went to the doctor and we learned that Sarah had tested positive for "Down-Syndrome". The doctors ran three separate tests and all three results were positive. Once again, we were faced with a trial. We didn't tell anyone about the doctor's visit and we certainly did not know what to expect.

A week later we were at our home eating dinner with pastor and his wife when two different cars pulled up. Eight to ten women got out of the cars and came and knocked on our door. Mary Alice B. stated that the women's group was praying at the church and felt like the Holy Spirit told them to come and pray for Lisa. One lady began to pray.

You could feel the battle raging in the spirit realm and it seemed nothing was happening.

Another lady, Deb Taylor, asked Lisa if she could kneel in front of her and put her hands on her belly. Lisa said that she could. Deb began to pray for Lisa. You could sense in the air something special. All of a sudden Deb began praying in an unknown language. Tongues were something we certainly were not used to and I wondered how Lisa was handling it. When I opened my eyes and looked over at Lisa I saw her belly moving around like an ocean wave. Sarah was moving and kicking like crazy. Lisa began crying and grabbing her stomach because she finally felt Sarah move in her belly after almost a week of no movement.

Lisa and I went back to the doctor's office and requested that more tests be done. The doctors ran the test and it was as we expected. Sarah was completely healed!!! GLORY!!!! What a mighty God we serve!

Eighteen months after Sarah was born, Rebekah was born in October of 1993. Even after being told we could not have children and after Lisa having a partial hysterectomy, we have a total of three great kids! Daniel, Sarah and Rebekah! Praise The Lord!

Chapter 2   **Walking on Trust Street**

When Lisa and I met I was a disc jockey for a local radio station. The day we got engaged I was actually laid off but I was still excited. I went to work at Moore's Lumber Co but got laid off in 1987. I then went to work at a clothing store as an assistant manager. I worked for a store called, "Jeans West" which later became "JW". A year later I was promoted and became the sales manager of that store.

I remember days when I would come home and tell my wife of the people I would catch shoplifting in the store and how much I would love to be a police officer. I would say things like, "Man, I wish I was a cop."

As I worked at the store, my regional manager was looking for me an Assistant Manager. Until he did I had to work 9am to 9pm six days a week and 11am to 6pm on Sundays. I literally did not have a day off for six months. Finally, I got an Assistant Manager at the store and my regional manager wanted to promote me again to a bigger store but I wasn't willing to relocate. My new Assistant Manager got the bigger store. Once again I was by myself, working with two part-time employees and no days off. I worked a total of nine months without a day off.

During that time I began to pray and ask God for help. I wouldn't suggest doing this unless you know absolutely sure the Holy Spirit is in this but I ended up resigning as manager of the retail store before I had another job lined up. The way I was working left me helpless and unable to look for another job because I was working 9am to 9pm daily.

Within a week I ended up getting a job as a mail runner for a local bank. I loved that job and met a great co-worker. Tim P. and I became close friends and we would pray together on our lunch hour, but my desire to become a police officer intensified. In September of 1990 I was praying and felt like the Holy Spirit told me to call around and ask if agencies were hiring. That's when I learned that Belle Police Department was hiring. When I called and asked them if they had any openings, the officer told me "yes", but tomorrow is the last day that we're accepting applications. He graciously agreed to meet me that evening at 5:30 and gave me an application. I filled it out and returned it the very next day before the 5pm deadline.

I was nervous about trying again for a police department. I had always wanted to be a police officer ever since I was 6 years old and I remember as a kid watching television shows like "Adam 12", "Andy Griffith", "Dragnet", "Starsky and Hutch", "Beretta", "Miami Vice" and the rest.

I had tried several times since I was 18 years old to become a police officer but I miserably failed every single time I took a test. Now at 24 years old, I was trying again. I remember praying and asking God, "Are you leading me? Is this what you want for me in my life?" I prayed, "God, if this job is mine and if you want me to be a police officer then please let me pass this test." I took the test for Belle Police Department in Belle, WV. I waited for what seemed like an eternity for the results to come back. Finally after waiting three or four weeks the results were posted. Parking the car, I told my wife again that if I pass, then I know God wants me in law enforcement but if I did not pass then God must not want me to be in law enforcement. I took a deep breath and walked over to the door where the results were posted.

I looked at the list and began to scan for my name. I think I actually started at the bottom hoping that my name at least made the bottom of the list. As I looked, I did not see it. I scrolled up…. and up….. FINALLY…… I found my name. I was third on the list. I had passed the test and I was third on the list. I was so thrilled I jumped for joy. I knew God wanted me to become a police officer.

But there were more tests to be done. I had to take a physical fitness test and I had to meet the city council and

Mayor. The process was long and drawn out. The process literally took months.

During this time I also had another job opportunity. My dad worked for DuPont Plant and had been there for years. My brother also worked there but he worked for a sub-contractor. I was currently making only $5.50 an hour so my brother and Dad told me I could get a job making almost double my current pay working for the sub-contractor with my brother. All I needed to do was go fill out the application so they could hire me.

I didn't want to disobey or be rude but I wanted to be a police officer so bad I could taste it. I had even passed the test so I believed that I had the job and God was guiding me. So, I did not fill out the form to work with my brother but he would encouraged me by saying that I would start out at $9 an hour and after 90 days I would be making as much as $12 an hour. That all sounded good especially since I was only making $5.50 but still my heart was to be a police officer.

In the months of waiting for the results of the tests, I remember getting more calls from concerned people who would be meaning well but would say things like, "You have a family to consider now", or "You have a child on the way that you have to think about". "Go get that job! What are you waiting for"?

I would explain to them that my heart really wanted this police job and that I had prayed and asked God to not let me pass the test if the job was not mine. One person asked, "How many took the test?" I said, "Twenty-six". They asked, "How many positions are they hiring?" I said, "One". The person said, "And you think you're it?"

I was hurt by that question but I knew the person was meaning well. I also knew in my heart how my Dad and Mom had raised me. My parents had raised me to follow

God no matter what. They raised me to pray and seek God's face in all things and that was exactly what I had in mind to do.

Following God isn't always easy and sometimes it can be right down difficult even to the point of losing friends. But following God is all there is. Nothing else matters!

I remember laying in bed one night about 11:30pm. I knew that what people were saying was right and I knew that they all meant well and were not trying to hurt my feelings. The deadline to fill out the application for my brother's work place was the next day so I was running out of time. Do I go take that job and just forget about the police job? After all, it was more money. Or do I hold on and trust God?

I called my pastor and explained to him what I was going through. Pastor asked me, "How bad do you want to do God's will?" I said, "Pastor, He's all I have." Pastor said, "I will call you back. I want to pray on this."

A few minutes later the phone rang. Again my pastor asked, "How bad do you want to do God's will?" Again, I told him, "He's all I have. I want to do only what God says to do." Pastor said, "I believe that if you hold on and not give in to pressure that God will help you."

I went to sleep that night with resolve in my heart that I was going to hold on a little longer for the police job. I knew the other job was going to be gone after tomorrow at 5pm but I didn't care. I was holding on.

Several weeks later I was on pins and needles. I didn't think this process was ever going to be over but word came down and I was in the top three candidates that were being considered for the police officer's job.

I was so excited but yet nervous. Finally, after four months of testing and waiting, I was told a selection was made and I would be getting a phone call soon.

I remember rushing home and sitting by the phone waiting for that phone call. Finally, the phone rang. I said, "Hello?" The voice said, "Randy, this is Bill C. and I'm the Mayor of the Town of Belle. I wanted to thank you for submitting your application with us. You were a great candidate and did extremely well on all the tests. But when it comes down to it, we've selected another man who has already been certified as a police officer. Thank you so much for your time."

I was crushed and devastated! I did not know what to do. Not only did I lose the police job, I had lost the job my brother and my dad had been telling me to go get for months before it was filled. I admit that I was really frustrated and I did not understand what had just happened. I thought God told me I had the job.

A few days went by but I never told my parents that I did not get the job. While I was at work I got a number on my pager so I called it back. It was a police officer from Belle

PD who told me he heard a rumor and said that I needed to get home as soon as I could and wait by the phone because I would be getting a call by 5pm.

Sure enough, as I got home and waited, I got another phone call. I said, "Hello?" The voice on the other end said, "Randy, this is Bill C. again, the Mayor of the Town of Belle. Are you still interested in working for us?" I said, "Yes, Sir I am." He said, "Good! One of the requirements we have is that you have to live inside the city within a year of being hired. The man we hired last week is not willing to do that because he just built his house and his wife does not want to move. Are you willing to move into town?" I said, "Yes, sir, I am!" He said, "Good! We'll see you in two weeks on a Monday morning. Welcome to Belle Police Department."

Three weeks after I became a police officer for the Town of Belle, I received a phone call. I was told, "You better be glad you didn't go to work for (that sub-contractor)." I asked, "Why?" I was then told that all of the men and women who worked there (including my brother) had been laid off with no hope of ever going back. In fact, my brother never did go back to work there ever again.

I thank God for His leadings! I praise Him for He was truly walking with me. Praise God, Praise God, Praise God!!! He worked it out!!!

Chapter 3   **My Life Spared**

As a police officer it is nice to believe that people would be praying for me. Lisa and I have a close friend named Joyce Burdette (Now Joyce Sader), who told me at church one night that God had called her to pray for me and that He made her my prayer warrior and she was going to be praying for my safety. I was thankful to hear that. What I didn't realize at the time was the significance of that statement and how true it was.

In April of 1993, I was on duty and was working the midnight shift. I was up on the four lane of Rt 60 looking for stranded motorists. This road was dark and there were no lights anywhere on the road and many times motorists would be stranded with no way to get to help.

As I traveled this four-lane road one night between 1:30am and 1:45am, I was making a legal U-Turn at Burning Springs. I immediately had a vision of my dad sitting beside me and it was like I was replaying what he said to me at 16 because he was saying the exact same thing to me.

Immediately the Holy Spirit spoke to me and said, "Son, get over in the right lane because there's a vehicle coming in your lane."

Allow me to insert something here..... When I was 16 years old, my dad taught me to drive a car. I remember one evening he was with me and said, "Son, never drive in the left lane of traffic because you never know when someone may jump the median and come at you head-on."

As I traveled this dark and lonely road I could tell there were no cars in my lane because there were no lights coming toward me. As I rounded a curve I looked up and I saw a car about quarter of a mile away from me but he was in his own lane. When the vehicle became closer to me, all of a sudden that vehicle jumped the concrete median and came toward me head-on. I moved my cruiser so far off the road that I was now up against the guard rail and had no place to go. Even if I tried to exit the passenger door of the car I would not have been able to because I was up so close against the rail.

That vehicle was heading straight for me and was not stopping. All I could do was say, "JESUS, HELP ME!" As soon as those words left my mouth the vehicle swerved and missed me literally by feet or inches. The vehicle continued and jumped back over the concrete median.

I turned on the blue lights and went after the vehicle. After I got the vehicle stopped, as expected, the driver was intoxicated. I arrested him and took him to jail approximately around 2:30am.

I got off duty that morning at 8am, went home, and went straight to bed not telling my wife the close encounter I had experienced.

Around 8:15 or 8:30am our house phone rang and Lisa answered the phone. I remember hearing her say, "Yes, he's in the bed. He just got home from nightshift." Then I heard her say, "Oh! Ok. Well hold on." Lisa then came into our bedroom and said, "Honey, this phone is for you. It's Joyce and she says it's very important that she talks to you before you go to sleep."

I took the phone and said, "Hello?" Joyce immediately said, "I want to know what happened to you last night?" Well this obviously peaked my curiosity so I asked her to repeat the question as I sat up in bed. She said, "I want to know what happened to you last night. But before you tell me, I want to tell you what happened to me last night." She continued and said, "About midnight last night the Holy Spirit woke me up and said, 'Go pray for Randy Myers'". She stated she laid there in bed and began to pray for me. But she stated the more she laid there and the more she tried to pray she could tell the Holy Spirit was frustrated with her and her prayers for me were going nowhere. She said,

"After about an hour of wrestling with God she asked, 'Lord what is it?' The Holy Spirit said, 'I said, **GO** pray for Randy Myers'". She said, "So, I got out of bed around 1am and I drove through town looking for your police car but I couldn't find you." She said, "I drove up and down every street and every alley looking for you but I couldn't find you." She said, "The burden was so great that I had to pull off the road because I was crying. I began to cry out to God for you and pray that God would protect you and spare your life. Finally at 2:30am I was released from this burden and I come back home and went to bed. Now, I want to know what happened to you last night."

Obviously, I was shocked at her words and I couldn't believe that our Heavenly Father would do that for me. I told her what had happened and told her she was able to go back to bed at 2:30am because that's when I was taking the man to jail.

Chapter 4 **Called To Leave**

In November of 1992, I was on duty and went to a park in the city down a small dead end road. I liked to go down there because it was usually quiet and I could pray, read my Bible and spend some time with God.

This particular evening I was doing my devotions and I felt in my heart that I heard the Holy Spirit talk to me in my inner self. This was very new to me and I did not really know what it was but I had this inner impression, "Son, I'm taking you out of Belle." When I looked up around me I could not believe my eyes. When I opened my eyes there were literally hundreds of doves surrounding my cruiser. Again the impression was strong, "You are leaving Belle, WV."

I told no one this. I knew I could not even tell my wife. My wife was and still is extremely close to her parents. If there was ever a "Momma's girl" she was it.

In December of 1992, I got up enough nerve to tell Lisa what I felt the Holy Spirit told me. In fact, I was nervous to talk to her, it is so vivid even still today that I can see and tell you exactly where we were when the conversation took place. We were both in our van going west bound on Rt 60 between the Malden Exit and the Campbell's Creek Exit. We were at the stop light of Campbell's Creek when Lisa said, "Well, you'll be going by yourself because I'm not going anywhere." I said, "Ok, honey" and left the conversation immediately.

Later that month Lisa and I traveled to Indianapolis, IN to go be with Rev Loran W Helm at an event called, "Waiting upon God". In this meeting there was an announcement of a trip to Israel. I had our babies in the over-flow section when that announcement came out and Lisa came running back and said, "Honey, wouldn't it be great if you got to go to Israel?" I said, "Oh, I would love to go but we can't afford that kind of money." My wife, with great faith said, "Well, If God wants you to go then He can provide the money.

Money is not an issue for Him." I became so excited about the possibility of going to Israel. In February of 1993 that dream came true. I was able to raise enough money to pay for the trip and go to Israel.

While I was in Israel I had such an experience there hearing God's voice. (We do not need to be in Israel to hear God's voice. We can hear Him no matter where we are on this earth.)

In our hotel one night, my roommate Mike F. and I were getting ready for the church service. It was really on my heart to hear a song by Daniel L. called, "Ordinary People". I mean it was so strong in my heart, I thought, "Lord, I would really like to hear Daniel L. sing that song."

Mike and I went to the church service and the next thing I knew, the Holy Spirit told Rev Helm that Daniel L. was to sing #5 on his list. Rev Helm did not even know what the song title was. So Daniel L. got up and began to sing #5 on his list...... It was "Ordinary People". Wow so amazing that God loves us so much that He would give us even the smallest desires of our heart.

Later in that same service another man was singing a song called, "In The Garden". As he sang the chorus:

> "And He walks with me and He talks with me and He tells me I am His own..."

When I heard that chorus immediately in my heart the Holy Spirit spoke with me and said, "You are my own." Joy filled my heart and I began to cry. And then sang it again:

> "And He walks with me and He talks with me and He tells me I am His own..."

Again in my heart I heard, "You are my own".

This was all new to me. I knew that we could talk to God all we wanted to but I did not know that God would speak to us this way. God was doing something new in me.

A couple of days later we were eating lunch and we began to leave. As the bus began to back up I looked out of the window and saw several sheep in a field. As we passed these sheep the Holy Spirit spoke to me and said, "My sheep hear me and know my voice. YOU are my sheep." Praise God! I am His sheep and I belong to the King! Hallelujah! Isn't it amazing that the God of the universe would speak to us this way if we just rest and listen to Him?

The next night, Mike F. and I were in our hotel and we were getting ready for church service. As Mike was getting ready, I felt the need to kneel at my bed and pray for the service. As I was praying, Mike came over and asked if he could pray with me.

I told Mike I knew in my heart that God was calling someone to come closer to Him so I was just praying for whoever that person may be. Mike began to pray with me and said, "…Lord, it could even be one of us…"

In the service, Rev Helm asked Ida K. to come and sing a song. It was a song I've never heard before or since. The song was called, "God Is My Goal". As soon as the first few words came out of her mouth I felt the Holy Spirit drawing me to go to the alter to pray. He was calling me to a deeper walk with Him. I sat there and was trying to refuse the call because I didn't know what it meant to "Surrender All". But I couldn't resist. I went to the altar and began to pray and tell God I surrender ALL to Him. I knew I was already saved and I knew that I was a Christian. But this call from God was a call to surrender all; A call to a deeper walk with Him.

As I got up from praying, I was met with hugs from several people. Once I got back to my seat Violinist, Maurice S.

began to play so beautifully on his violin and the congregation began to sing, "And He walks with me and He talks with me and He tells me I am His own." God was telling me once again that I was His own.

On February 14th we were still in Israel. Mike and I were missing our wives very much. We knelt by our beds in our hotel room and we began to pray for our wives that God would send them our love on this Valentine's Day. We had been in Israel about five days and we had not been able to call them. As Mike and I were praying, God gave me a vision of my wife lying in bed. She was crying because she missed me so much. It was the first time she and I had been separate since I was in the police academy for 13 weeks.

I called Lisa later that night about 11:30pm Jerusalem time. I wished her a "Happy Valentine's Day". I asked how she was doing and I told her that I saw her lying across our bed and crying. She said, "How did you know that?" I didn't know that except the Holy Spirit showed me.

The next day, we were eating lunch and I was eating with some people from Florida who were with us on our trip to Israel. Brian B. began to share his story with me about how God had moved him from place to place. As he spoke to me things were going on in my heart that I never experienced before. I thought maybe God was "confirming" in me what Brian was saying but as we were leaving the place we ate I knew in my heart that God was telling me, "You are leaving Belle, WV".

I couldn't wait to call Lisa and tell her. The feeling in my heart was so strong that it was almost overwhelming. I couldn't wait so I called Lisa again that night from Jerusalem, Israel. I surprised her with a second call. All I said to her was, "Honey, when I get home we really need to talk." She said, "We're not moving are we?" I said, "Honey, I've been in Israel for over a week. I could talk to you about anything here. What in the world possessed you to say that?" She said, "I do not know except that all day I've had this overwhelming feeling we are leaving this town." I said, "Well do you know then where we are going because I don't." She said, "No, but I know now that God is asking us to leave and I am willing to go wherever you choose to go." HALLELUJAH!!! What a mighty God we serve!

A few more days went by and we began our journey back to the United States. We landed in NY and then flew to Charlotte, NC.

Lisa and I were so excited about what God was doing with us but we were nervous because we didn't know where we were going. You could sense the presence of God in the hotel room as we talked about moving and leaving Belle.

As Lisa and I sat in the van we were waiting for our pastor and his wife to come so we could go to a church service. I saw them approaching and said, "Honey, let us not say a word about this to anyone here. We don't know where we're going or even when. I don't want to look like a fool."

As we traveled to the church, Lisa and our pastor began talking about how some of her family members were hurt by a church they were attending in another city. All of a sudden, Pastor turned completely around in the front seat of the van, looked at Lisa and said, "You know Lisa, God may move you and Randy out of state to reach (those people)." I could not believe my ears. He knew nothing of what we were going through. Lisa and I still never said a word but I just kept driving. The next day we went back home to Belle, WV.

A month and a half later I received a phone call from our pastor who requested that I come to his house because there was something he needed to tell me. When I arrived at his house, my close friend and brother in Christ, Mark Skiles was already there. Mark and I were two of the three board members of the church at that time. I wasn't sure what was going on but I knew it was something serious.

Pastor made a conference call to a third member of the board who couldn't be at the house for the meeting. It was then that our pastor announced that he would be leaving Maranatha Outreach Center. He stated that God was leading him to Clinton, TN. I couldn't believe what I was hearing. I was devastated. All I could think was I was losing my best friend who I believed was a true man of God. A man who had been teaching me things I never knew about in the Kingdom of God for the last three and half years. I was so crushed I couldn't say a word. I left the meeting and immediately went home. When I entered our house from the back door Lisa asked, "So, when is Pastor leaving?" I couldn't even answer her. How did she know such a thing? I just found out only five minutes ago. I walked right passed her and went straight down to the basement where I cried out to God in prayer. Lisa told me later that I sounded like a dog howling in pain.

But as I was in prayer, my mind racing and asking God why this was to be. I actually felt God Himself bend over from heaven, get close to my right ear and whispered, "But this is my will." As I cried, I said, "I know." A few seconds after I said, "I know" the Holy Spirit quickened me. It was like there was a light bulb that went off over the top of my head. Could it be? Could it really be?

I ran upstairs in to the kitchen where Lisa was. I said, "Honey, do you get it? Do you get it? We are called to be with pastor and his wife! We are called to be with them! This is the thing that God has been telling us since November of last year." Lisa looked at me with amazement. Could it be true?

Months had long passed and pastor and his wife had already been gone since May of 1993. Our other closest friends, Mark and Robin Skiles had also left WV in June to be in TN. Lisa and I was still in Belle, WV. We traveled to Clinton, TN almost every month for about two years as I tried several times to get a job with a police department there but none considered me.

We made the mistake of telling people prematurely that we would be leaving WV and that we felt God calling us to be with our pastor in TN. We told them all I needed to do was get a job there and we were leaving. As it turned out God had other plans first. So when things didn't go as planned, people started having "concerns" about me hearing from God because bad things began to happen.

In November 1993, we were still in WV and our landlord had passed away. Lisa and I felt for sure that this was it. God would be opening up the doors for us in TN and we would be moving. But that did not happen.

In January 1994, Lisa and I received a certified letter in the mail. The letter was from our landlord's daughter and she requested that we vacate the house. She explained in the letter that her father gave her the house in his will and she wanted to move in to the house so we had to leave.

As more weeks and months went passed, I looked for housing for my family but could not find any. Belle is an extremely small town and there were not a lot of housing to choose from. I called the lady and explained to her that it was mandatory for me to live inside the city limits if I were to be a police officer in Belle. I told her that I was trying the best I could but there were no other houses or apartments that I could rent. I even told her my wife had just had our third child who was still an infant and we had no place to go. The lady said she did not care about my woes and that we needed to get out of her house.

We thought for sure God would have opened the door for us to move to TN by now. Could He not see our dilemma that we were in? Did He not care we were going to be homeless unless He helped us?

In April of 1994, Lisa and I had to move from Belle, WV but it was not to TN. In fact, this began one of the hardest journeys of our life.

Lisa and I moved into a home with close friends, Bill and Karen G. in Charleston, WV. They were so gracious and kind to open up and share their home to us. We were eternally grateful for the hospitality. You could sense the presence of God in their home.

A month went by and I remember sitting in the living room and there were some other close friends who had come by to encourage Lisa and me. We were talking about the love of God even though we were in a hard place and that God still had His hand on us.

Daniel was sitting on my lap. At the age of three years old you could tell that he loved his daddy and would be with me everywhere I was. This night as he sat on my lap listening to our conversation, Daniel looked up at me and said, "Daddy, I want to ask Jesus in my heart." I was amazed. I did not know the Holy Spirit could speak to babies so young. But we all prayed in the living room of this home. When we were done praying, Daniel began preaching in his baby talk. We couldn't understand a word he was saying but you knew the Holy Spirit was on him as his face was red and his little veins were popping out of his neck. It was an amazing site to behold. Even in our time of struggle God was giving us nuggets along the way to tell us that He was with us.

After two months of living with our friends, Lisa and I moved in with family members. We still had not heard anything from TN and we did not want to continue to be a burden on Bill and Karen any longer so we moved.

During this time in our lives the battles were so intense at times. It was bad enough not having a place to call our own home but also hard on me as a husband and as a father. I felt like a complete failure at times. If it wasn't for our friends, Bill and Karen and also Joyce and Lester B., I don't know what Lisa and I would have done.

There were occasions when concerned people would question us and say, "I thought you said God told you, you all were leaving Belle and going to Tennessee?" There were times when things got so heated that concerned people in our lives would hold our children in their arms, point their finger in my wife's face and say, "And you call yourself a mother?"

All we could do was just wait and trust in our God who was guiding us. We had no control over the situation as it were. We could not understand why things were not opening up for us in TN and at the same time we could not control the fact that we were told to leave our house in Belle at no fault of our own.

In November of 1994, Lisa and I moved to South Charleston, WV. The man who rented to us was a man of

God and did not require us to sign a year's lease. We told him our situation and explained to him that we were in transition and believed that God was leading us to Tennessee. He told us this house sat empty for five months because God had told him earlier that a family would need it. He believed we were that family.

Lisa and I continued to travel to Tennessee every month to be with our friends, Mark and Robin Skiles and our former pastor and his wife.

In the spring of 1995, I was able to take a test for the Anderson County Sheriff's Office and I passed their test.

By early August of 1995, we still had not heard anything from the sheriff's office or any other agency in TN, so Lisa and I went on vacation with her parents to Myrtle Beach, SC. We left on a Saturday and were going to be staying until the following Saturday.

I remember waking up on a Wednesday morning around 7:30am and the Holy Spirit told me to call our former pastor. I felt it was a little early to call so I waited and called around 8:30am. When I called, his wife answered the phone and I asked if I could speak to pastor. She stated he was gone to Indiana and wouldn't be back for a few days.

In my mind I didn't understand that because I knew the Holy Spirit told me to call. I also knew that God is an all knowing God and He knew pastor was not at home when He told me to call. As these thoughts were going through my head, his wife said, "Who is this? Randy is this you?" I said, "It is." She said, "Where are you? I've been trying to get a hold of you for three days. The Sheriff of Anderson County has been calling here looking for you and he wants you to call him back as soon as you can."

Think of that! The Holy Spirit knew where I was and spoke to me and told me to call pastor so I could actually get a message from his wife! Hallelujah to the Lamb for His mercy and His grace!

I got the number I was to call and called the Sheriff's office immediately. When I called, I spoke to D. M. who had been such a great help to me in getting to the test site and getting my paper work into the office as they needed it. She knew that the Sheriff had been looking for me and transferred me to him instantly.

The Sheriff told me he liked my application and test scores and he wanted to interview and possibly hire me. He wanted to know how soon I could come to TN. I told him we would be there the next day and that he could interview me on Friday.

I hung up the phone and told Lisa what had just happened. She was thrilled and yet nervous. Lisa and I cut our vacation short and left Myrtle Beach the very next day and drove 9 hours to Clinton, TN.

The next day I met the Sheriff and a few other administration officers. The Sheriff hired me on the spot and wanted me to start right away. By God's grace and divine intervention, Lisa and I moved to Clinton, TN by the end of August of 1995. Praise the Lord.

Even through adversity and even though the journey was hard and difficult, God had helped us to become debt free before He moved us. Through this time in our life, God showed us that He was still with us and true to His Word that we were to move out of Belle, WV and come to Clinton, TN.

As you obey the Holy Spirit, people may not like, understand, or even agree with why you do the things you do but the important thing is just OBEY.

Chapter 5   **A Different World**

The first three weeks working for the sheriff's office was a learning experience for me. There were obvious cultural differences between where I had been to where I am now, but I had a good Sergeant and a good FTO (Field Training Officer).

One night, there were four of us in a parking lot on the corner of Raccoon Valley Road and Clinton Hwy talking when we saw a vehicle stop in the middle of the road before turning onto Edgemoor Rd. The driver of this vehicle apparently did not see us. He got out of his vehicle and urinated in the middle of the road. The Sergeant said to my FTO, "Take Randy and you two go check on that guy down there."

So, Deputy P. W. and I got in our police car and I drove to the corner. When I pulled up behind the vehicle and turned on the blue lights to stop him the chase was on. The vehicle sped down Edgemoor Rd doing over 100 mph. To make things more dangerous, it began to sprinkle rain.

The chase continued into Oak Ridge and then back into Clinton where this wanted felon rammed a Clinton Police Officer in his cruiser. Thankfully, Sgt J. H. of Clinton PD was not injured and was able to get the vehicle stopped. It turned out that the driver of the fleeing vehicle had seven felony warrants on him in Knox County.

While I was directing traffic and waiting for the wrecker to come and pick up the suspect's car, I remember hearing something coming behind me. I then saw a man walking towards me who seemingly came out of "nowhere". When I looked at him I noticed he had fatigues on and his face was painted green and black like the military does when they are in the woods. You can imagine how I felt seeing this man walking up on me at 2:00am just after what had happened in the middle of the road. Apparently, it was pretty obvious to this person, too, that it unnerved me because he laughed and said, "It's ok buddy, I'm a police officer too." and shows me his badge. This officer was a Clinton officer conducting surveillance at the time of the wreck and came to assist his fellow officer.

I couldn't believe all that had just happened. I had been a police officer for five years and not had anything so wild to take place like that. My first five years in the little town of Belle was quiet. In fact, Belle was so quiet and peaceful its nick-name was, "Mayberry" because nothing ever happened there. I remember, just after I was hired there, the former Chief of Police stating that he had been there for 27 years and never even pulled his gun in the line of duty. Now, just three weeks with my new agency I'm in a high speed chase with a drunken wanted felon who was using the streets for their bathroom. After he rams a police car three times, then wrecks out I have "Rambo" coming out of nowhere scaring me to death.

I remember thinking, "God, what have you gotten me into?"

The next week I was back on duty again still with my FTO. Dispatch sent me on a call to the hospital to pick up a male subject and take him to a mental hospital in Knoxville. Since there were only four deputies in three cruisers, I had to go by the jail first and get my own cruiser.

As I was getting in the cruiser in front of the jail, Sgt Z.B. came out and began talking to me. He asked what I was doing. I told him that I have to go to the hospital and pick up someone and take him on to Knoxville. Sgt. Z. B. had a look of concern in his eye and said, "Are they sending you by yourself?" I said, "Yes sir." He said, "Do you know who you are going after?" I said, "No sir." He said, "Wait right here." The Sergeant then comes back out of the jail carrying leg irons and shackles. He says, "Here, take these. The last time we dealt with this man he fought us and it took nine of us to get him down." I thought, "That's just great, God. You move me down here to TN and kill me within a month." Needless to say, I prayed all the way to the hospital.

When I walked through the door of the hospital my eyes immediately came fixed on a man who reminded me of Charles Manson. (For those of you who do not know who that is; Manson is in prison today for mass murder.) I was hoping he was not the one I was there to get but sure enough, the nurse informs me that was him.

I walked into the room and the man immediately began to "size me up". I looked back at him in his eyes and told him we could do this the easy way or the hard way. The choice was his. He was compliant and allowed me to put the handcuffs and shackles on him and walk him out to my cruiser.

When we were on our way to the other hospital this man began talking to himself. He then looked at me through my rearview mirror and asked the question, "Why can't I die?" He would ask that repeatedly. The more he asked the louder he became. The more he became louder the more I would turn up the music on the radio. He would get louder so I would turn up the music louder.

All the way down Pellissippi Hwy he would keep yelling and asking, "Why can't I die?" As best I could I tried to ignore him but finally I had all I could take. As he was yelling in the back seat, "Why can't I die?" I reached up and turned the music completely off and I said, "FINE! You want me to tell you why you can't die?" He leaned up toward the back of the cage and said, "Yeah! Tell me!" I said, "Because two thousand years ago Jesus Christ died on the cross for you so you don't have to die!" The man did not know what to say. All he could say was, "Oh."

I began to share about the love of Jesus to this man. While going down the interstate, this man said the sinner's prayer and gave his heart to Jesus.

Years later when I saw him again, he told me that when I first walked into the hospital he had every intension of fighting me but he knew there was something different about me. I do not know where this man is today but I do know that night he had an encounter with Jesus.

Chapter 6   **Calls For Service**

In The Heavenly Realm

Throughout the next few years God seemed to still have his hand on me. As I look back now, I can see times when he was guiding me and directing my path and even directing me in calls for service.

Many nights while on duty God's hand of protection was upon me. Other times He would send me to calls where I would be able to share the love of God with people; maybe not so much in words but in actions.

On May 27, 1996, I was sent to check on the well being of a man who was threatening suicide. One of the first words out his mouth was, "I just want to end it all. It's not worth it here anymore." Reserve Deputy Lynn Cox and I began to talk with this man. We tried to give him hope and encouragement. We found out that this man used to be a minister of the Gospel in a Baptist Church but Satan had gotten a hold of him and now he was using cocaine and he had become an alcoholic.

The man looked at us and said, "You guys are shooting straight from the hip aint ya. You got me thinking."

We were able to get this man some help. I don't know where he is today but I'm thankful that a seed was planted in his heart. Most importantly, he did not commit suicide.

In the early morning hours of June 1, 1996, Deputy Cox and I were again together. It was great having a Christian brother riding with me. God seemed to guide our calls and get us to the right place at the right time on several occasions.

On this particular night we were dispatched to a family disturbance. Family members were able to take the weapons away from a man who stated he wanted to commit suicide. When we arrived on the scene this man was saying, "I just want it all to end."

It's amazing how the devil uses the same feelings and the same lines to get people down. He knows no new tricks. It's the same things over and over again. I've learned throughout my twenty plus years as a police officer that people really do not want to kill themselves. They just want the pain to stop.

Deputy Cox and I began to encourage this man and talk with him about his troubles and try to find out what was going on with him. At one point he looked at me and said, "You've meant more to me in this little bit of time than my dad has meant to me my whole life."

We were able to talk to this man into going to the hospital to be checked out. On our way there, I felt the Holy Spirit rise up in me and I said to this man, "Sir, you need to stop running from your calling. You are called to preach aren't you?" He said, "How did you know that? I've been running from that for two years and I've never told anyone that. How did you know that?"

I didn't……. The fact is I don't know anything unless the Holy Spirit shows me.

On September 13, 1997, I was working a side job as ninety-nine percent of police officers do. On this date I was working a football game on a Saturday afternoon in Claxton, TN.

After the game was over there was a kid acting silly like most kids do trying to have some fun. He was on my left and his grandmother was on my right. His mother walked up and his grandmother said, "You need to get your son" as she pointed in my direction. The mother did not see her son on the other side of me and thought her mom was talking about me. Then seeing her son, she laughed and said, "I thought you were talking about this officer and he is not my son." We laughed and I said, "Why? Don't you claim me?" She said, "No, it's not that. You already claimed me on Mehaffey Road one night." At first, I did not remember this lady but she remembered me. She continued to tell me, "One night after midnight about a year and a half ago, you pulled me over." The story goes that after I pulled her over she was sitting in the front seat of my cruiser (which is something I've only done twice in my career). When this lady was sitting in the front seat of my cruiser she heard my music playing and a conversation came up about God. She began to tell me how bad things were in her life and that she had this problem and that problem. About the time she was sharing her problems with me a song came on the radio...... "There Is No Problem Too Big That God Cannot Solve It". I began to smile when I heard the music start because I knew what was about to be sung. I turned up the radio and told her to listen to the words of this song.

There is no problem too big, God cannot solve it.

There is no mountain so tall He cannot move it.

There is so no storm so dark God cannot calm it.

There is no sorrow so deep, He cannot sooth it.

If He carried the weight of the world upon His shoulder,

I know my brother that He can carry you.

If He carried the weight of the world upon His shoulder,

I know my sister, that He can carry you.

As we listened to that song on the radio, I remember that I told her that was no coincidence and God was speaking to her through the radio.

As this lady stood beside me and reviewed this story with me at the football field that Saturday afternoon, she went on to say, "I just wanted you to know that I gave my life to Jesus and I am back in church now." Praise the Lord!

I'm thankful for the leadings of the Holy Spirit. We as Christians really do need to have a relationship with God and just be with Him. He has so much to tell us and show us. There are people all around us who need a touch from God. A lot of times we do not have to do a thing. God will do all the work. All we have to do is be faithful. With that we must remember and realize that we cannot save anyone. The Bible says that no one comes to the Father unless the Holy Spirit draws him, but we can be a witness for Him. Some plant, some water and some reap. Be a planter and one who waters. Let God do the reaping and use you in the process.

Francis of Assisi said, "Preach the Word always! Use words if you must."

If we will be faithful to God and have a relationship with Him, He will use our walk more than He'll use our words, but words without the walk is meaningless.

Chapter 7   Angel Of Life

On February 16, 1997, I was at home getting ready to go on duty. I had such a sick feeling on me that I could hardly walk. I physically would have to bend over at times because the burden was so heavy. I went to my bed room and knelt at the foot of my bed and began to cry out to God and asked Him what He was trying to tell me. It was almost unbearable. As I prayed I felt like this was a burden of death.

I cried out to God for mercy, then had a sense that I needed to ask my Sergeant if I could change zone assignments with my partner. So, early in the shift I obtained permission to do just that. I did not understand why. I just knew that I had to change zones.

I was patrolling the south part of the county and the night was extremely quiet. There were hardly any calls for service that night. But, at 1:26 am, while I was patrolling the streets of Edgemoor Rd and Clinton Hwy Clinton City dispatched their fire department to a house fire. According to the call, there were still two people trapped inside. As Clinton dispatched the call, I heard a female screaming in the background.

I started toward Clinton. A short time after the original dispatch, I heard Sgt. M. M. key his mic and again a female screaming in the background. Sgt. M. M. stated that there were two subjects still inside the residence. I responded to the scene.

After I arrived at the scene, I heard glass breaking as I exited my vehicle and started toward the house. The smoke from the fire had already covered the area. Approaching the house I began looking through the windows of the basement to see if I could see anyone.

As I was going around the house an officer from Clinton began to yell, "I've got a body! I've got a body!" Officer

G.G. was by a window that was ground level. I ran to him and tried to look in the window but I could not see anything because of the thick black smoke. About that time, Capt. J. L. from the Clinton Fire Department came over to assist.

At first, he could not see anything, but Officer G.G. and I continued to shine our flashlights into the room pointing toward the body. When Capt. J. L. noticed the body, he moved with vigor and quickly kicked out the window frame keeping us from reaching the child. Capt. J. L. jumped down into the basement. I couldn't believe how fast he got in there. It was almost as if he dove in head first.

A puff of black smoke rolled out of the window, covered Officer G.G.'s face and choked him so he had to leave the window. I took his place. At that time I saw the small foot of a child. Capt. J. L. picked up the child and tried to hand him to me but he fell backward. Smoke rolled out of the window covering my face and glasses. I could not see through them so I threw them to the side.

Capt. J. L. got up with the child and lifted him up to me so he could be pulled out from the burning house. Officer G. G. and I ran with the child away from the house and placed him on the ground. There was no pulse or heartbeat and the child was not breathing. As I looked at the child, his face was covered with black smoke - a tar looking substance was coming from the boy's nostrils. I couldn't help but think of my own son, Daniel, who was only six years old at the time.

Officer G. G. began yelling, "God help me, help me God!" I didn't care who was around, I began to pray out loud as I was wiping the black smoke off of the child's face and tried to help Officer G. G. clear the child's mouth of the black tar looking substance.

Trying to move as careful, but as swiftly as possible, Officer G. G. and I began CPR. With every breath given, you could hear a gurgling sound in the lungs. In between breaths and chest compressions, the child's mouth needed to be cleared.

At one point, the boy's teeth clamped down on Officer G. G.'s fingers. He had to use his other hand to pry the boy's mouth open to free the hand that was bitten as he said, "Oh, don't bite me son," and continued to work.

It seemed as though the CPR was doing no good, but Sgt. D. H. of Anderson County Sheriff's Office was by our side encouraging us to keep going.

Finally, we detected a heartbeat and the child gasped for air - two more breaths were given. Asst. Fire Chief L. M. picked up the child, threw him over his shoulder and we began to run around to the back of the house where the ambulance was. As we ran, the pressure on the child's stomach from the Asst Chief's shoulder caused more of the tar like substance to gush from the child's mouth down his back.

Arriving around back and placing the child back on the ground, we wrapped him in blankets. I was handed an ambo bag which I placed on the child's face and continued to breathe for the child as the medics placed heart monitors and other items on him. Using my flashlight, paramedic H. K. began to check the eyes of the child - the eyes responded.

While we were still working on the child I had to move slightly. When I did my guardian angel pin fell off of my jacket collar and on to the boy's chest. I stopped squeezing the ambo bag to pick up my angel pin and put it in my jacket pocket.

When I placed my hand back on the bag, I noticed the child's chest rise and fall by itself. It was as if the angel had breathed new life into the boy. The boy was now breathing on his own! With joy I alerted H. K. to the fact. He was pleased, but said to keep going so I did.

As we continued to work with the child, I heard my partner radio in to dispatch that he was enroute to the scene. If I would not have switched zone assignments with him at the beginning of the shift I would not have been there at that moment in time.

Officer G. G. was rubbing the boy's body to help keep him warm so he wouldn't go into shock. We both kept praying and talking to the child telling him to hang on and that he was doing really well. At one point, while rubbing his head, I leaned down to the boy's ear and said, "I don't know if you can hear me, but if you can... just trust Jesus, OK?' Just trust Jesus!"

Soon after that, we all picked the child up and placed him on the cot so we could get him to the helicopter that was on the way.

Once in the ambulance, I put the oxygen mask on the boy and just kept talking to him. Still paramedics were working with him doing whatever was needed.

I continued to talk to him and look into his eyes to see if they were still reacting to the lights. They were. I didn't notice at this time that the boy had eye contact with me. The paramedic beside me noticed the boy's eyes and said, "keep talking to him Randy, he's looking at you, he has eye contact with you." I kept talking and rubbing the boy's head. Finally, the helicopter arrived and we rushed the boy from the ambulance to the "Life Star" helicopter.

While running and pushing the cot to the helicopter, the child raised his arm and grabbed mine. This was the first real motion to show signs of life. As we walked back to the ambulance, Officer G. G. looked at me and shook my hand and said, "God was with us!" I said, "Yes, God had mercy on us." As we got into the back of the ambulance to return to the scene I began to cry only now realizing the reality of everything going on.

Arriving back at the fire scene, Sgt. D. H. requested that I come to the jail. When I arrived I noticed that the Sheriff was there along with Capt. A. J. and Sgt. D. H. I walked through the lobby door and Sgt. D. H. shook my hand and said, "I want you to know, you did a good job out there." The Sheriff then asked about the boy and I told him what I knew.

As Sgt. D. H. and the Sheriff were talking I asked, "What is going on?" The Sheriff looked at me and said, "Don't you know? That is one of our officer's house that is on fire. That was his wife and son in the house. You didn't know who that was?" I said, "No, I had no idea."

It was then that I learned the child's name and that he was only nine years old. This information stunned me and shook me up even more. I had no clue the call I was on involved one of my own co-workers.

The Sheriff asked me to share the news with the dad about his son. Until this time he knew nothing except that his house was on fire. I went into the room and told him what I knew about his son. He hugged me and said, "Thanks for everything you've done." He then left to go to the hospital to see his family. Later the phone rang. My co-worker's wife had passed away.

I went to the Clinton Police Department. The Clinton dispatcher told me that the "Life Star" helicopter medics had radioed back and said, "Tell the two police officers that they saved the boy's life." Jesus did in fact help us and He answered our prayers.

A debriefing was held that same night. Everyone involved in the rescue attempt was told to be there. It was at this debriefing I learned that "seconds or minutes" after we pulled the child from the window, that twelve foot flames shot out of the same window where we were. According to Assistant Fire Chief L. M., the flames went so high that it burned and melted the eves on the roof of the house.

I also learned the story of one of the helicopter medics, Robert B. Robert said that he wasn't supposed to work that night, but felt like God had wanted him to, so he did. While enroute to the hospital, he gave the child some medicine. He said he had only seconds to make a decision because he could not get the tube down the child's throat because it was so swollen. He had to make the decision whether or not to give him a tracheotomy to help him to breath. He said that something told him "...to try one more time..." to get the tube down the boy's throat. He said, "Folks you just don't do that, but I tried one more time and the tube went down so easy. Nothing blocked it." You could tell Robert was amazed. Robert gave all of the credit to God.

Two weeks after the fire, the child walked out of the University of Tennessee Hospital on his own power. My wife and I had the privilege of being a witness of that. He is still alive and well today because of our God -- Jesus Christ!

Matthew 19:26 says, "...With men this is impossible; but with God all things are possible."

Chapter 8   God's Mercy & Protection

One Saturday morning around 6:30am I was on my way home from working midnight shift. As I was traveling down Ridgeview Drive (a VERY hilly road) the Lord spoke to my heart and said, "Son, slow down." I looked at my speedometer and I was only doing 15 to 20 mph in a 35mph zone because of a sharp curve. I thought that was strange so I began to do the speed limit as the road straightened out. Again, I heard, "Son, you need to slow down." Thinking I was losing my mind I began to slow down anyway.

As I slowed the Lord kept prompting me, "Slower." "Slower." I slowed down so much that I was now stopped in the middle of the road near the South Clinton Football Field at 6:30 in the morning with no other vehicles on the road (or so I thought).

As I was sitting there wondering what I was doing, a truck came up to the intersection on the other side of the field on Unika St. Not knowing what I was doing the truck began to pull out. As he did another vehicle was coming towards us but in its own lane. The road was so hilly that you could not see if any vehicles were coming. So the truck began to pull out into this dangerous intersection and the oncoming car had to swerve into my lane to miss hitting that truck. The car then went out of control and began sliding sideways in my lane (the car by all rights should have flipped over). Somehow, the driver of the car regained control and missed the front of my cruiser by a few feet.

A short distance down the road, I turned my blue lights on and stopped the truck to see if the driver was intoxicated. As I exited my patrol car I smelled alcohol coming from his vehicle. I said, "Sir, have you been drinking?" He said, "No Sir, I am a minister from Sevierville, TN and I was called by this man (a passenger in the vehicle) to take him home because he had too much to drink". I said, "Sir, do you know that God spared us back there?" He said, "I sure do." After a brief conversation the man went on his way.

One week later I was in my church at Clinton Christ Fellowship and I felt the need to share this story to the congregation. So I did. I started out by saying, "I want to thank God for HIS protection..." and I told the church this story. When I sat down a lady who sat across the isle from me stood up and said, "I too, want to thank God for HIS protection because that was me in that car."

The lady that stood was our pastor's sister-in-law and a very good friend of my family. She said, "I lost all control of that car and I don't know how I got it back. I was on my way to work and was wondering why a police car was sitting in the middle of the road at 6:30 in the morning. Now I know."

Praise the Lord for HIS protection and for HIS mercy. God in HIS wonderful way spared three lives that morning. Had

I not listened to the Holy Spirit I would have hit that car in the driver's door and possibly killed the driver, whom I learned later was my good friend.

Even if and when we do not understand "why"; Even when it does not make sense, if we are faithful to God He will guide us and protect us from things we know nothing of. It was very hard for me to sit there in the middle of the road for those few seconds (especially on a Saturday morning with no one on the road) but had the Holy Spirit not spoke; someone may have been hurt or killed.

I GIVE JESUS ALL THE PRAISE AND GLORY!!!!

Chapter 9

Learning Obedience

(Florida Trips)

In 1997, God had been speaking to me about starting a ministry for police officers for several months. In 1998, He then began to "show" me when He lead us on a trip to Florida. My mentor and friend Chief Jack Rinchich had written some tracks for police officers and I would share them as the Holy Spirit prompted.

In May 1998, I believed the Holy Spirit lead us to go on vacation with two close friends of ours. (Lead on King Jesus! I wish that happened every year.) My family and I along with Stephen and Michelle Carpenter drove to Ft. Lauderdale, Florida.

On the way to Florida it seemed as though every time we stopped we would come in contact with a police officer. We stopped in SC at a Shoney's Restaurant and came in contact with a former Police Chief and were able to share the tracks with him and witness to him. When we arrived in Winter Garden, FL we saw a stranded motorist on the side of the road with four occupants. I do not suggest that you always stop to assist motorists, but I believed the Holy Spirit told me to stop and check on the occupants of the vehicle. It turned out to be an off duty police officer with his wife along with two other correctional officers. I was able to share Jack's tracks with them.

We spent the night in Winter Garden, FL before heading on to Ft. Lauderdale. We woke up the next morning and went to eat breakfast and again, we came in contact with three more police officers and I gave them the tracks. In less than twenty-four hours the Holy Spirit had lead me to seven police officers.

As we were doing what we believed to be right, it seemed as though God was teaching us about walking in obedience.

We arrived in Ft. Lauderdale. The kids were so excited about being at the beach. We unpacked then Lisa took the kids by the pool.

The next evening, after being by the pool we went to our rooms to rest. Not long after Lisa and I got our room our phone rang. It was Michelle and she asked for prayer because she had gotten sick from the time she left us until the time she got to her room. I thought that was kind of quick so I suggested that she was burdened. She asked that Lisa and I come over to their room for prayer so we did.

We arrived in their room and Michelle was trying to explain to Stephen her burden. Stephen had walked up separately from Michelle and had said that as he walked around the building he too got a burden. He said he believed he heard in his spirit, "Lower level danger".

Through prayer we believed God was warning us about a danger. The word was to stay out of the ocean. That was difficult to hear because that's what we were there for. Were we going to obey or just think it was silly not to be able to get into the ocean?

Two days later, Lisa and I were at the pool with the kids and Lisa met a lady who had rash all over her body. She looked to be in a lot of pain with her neck and face swollen. Lisa asked her what happened and the lady told her she did not know but she felt sick. She said the only thing she did different than her family members was she got into the ocean. I believe God spared us from whatever made that lady sick from the ocean.

A few days later we believed God lead us to a restaurant to eat. I believed in my heart that God wanted us to meet the waitress that was to serve us. We arrived at the restaurant but the only table open was one in the smoking section. That was not my choice but felt it was right so we sat at the table. Before we left a friend of mine began to witness to the waitress. She was telling us about her boyfriend who was going to be her husband. As she spoke I believed God gave me a burden for this man. It turned out that he was a police officer thus the reason for my burden.

The whole trip to Florida seemed to be surrounded by police officers both on and off duty. Every time we turned around one would cross our path.

We did not know it at the time, but God was teaching us about walking in obedience. When we are walking obedience to HIM we unlock miracles. We see things we would not have ever seen. We are spared from the things that would have hurt us and at the same time, we are able to encourage other people and make them feel lifted in their spirit.

The next year, we were eating and sharing with others about how God lead us to Florida and to all of the officers we ultimately met. As we were sharing those stories, God began to speak to me and I believed He told me we were going to go back Florida one day soon.

Lisa and I talked about going back that summer but the finances just did not seem to be there for us. In our minds, we determined not to go, but God had other plans.

I was praying one day and the Holy Spirit spoke to me and said, "Leave May 22nd." I did not share this with anyone because of the decision Lisa and I made, NOT to go this year. Approximately three days later, I received a phone call from Michelle Carpenter. She was praying and the Holy Spirit told her we were to, "leave May 22nd." I have to admit, I was a bit shocked.

Realizing that God was moving, I told Lisa we would commit to going to Florida again and we would trust God for the finances to come.

Three weeks before we left, we received a check in the mail for $800.

While we were planning the trip the question came, "Do we drive straight through or do we stop half way to sleep?" Through prayer and counsel, we believed the Holy Spirit was leading us to drive straight through. I knew that would be difficult because our kids were less than ten years old. For us, it was a continuation of training and learning obedience.

At 6:30am on May 22nd, my family along with Stephen and Michelle loaded up and headed back to Ft. Lauderdale Florida. Fourteen and half hours later we made it. The kids did great! They never complained one time.

84

We arrived at the hotel and learned that our room was on the 15th floor. If you know anything about me, you know that I hate heights but if I can look out and not down, it isn't as bad on me. When went into the room, I place my bags on the floor in the bedroom. I went over to the window and opened the curtains to look out to the ocean. When I did, I immediately got this sick feeling and felt as though someone or some *thing* grabbed me pulling me through the window. Freaked out, I closed the curtains back and walked away without saying a word.

Several minutes later, everyone was at the pool talking and Lisa told Stephen and Michelle what happened to me and then I found out, that right behind me, my daughter Sarah, looked out the window and immediately got sick as well. Stephen spoke up and said he looked out his window too and got sick.

It didn't take us long to figure out that God was trying to tell us something. I helped Lisa put the kids to bed and I went to Stephen and Michelle's room for prayer. While we were praying you could sense something wasn't right. The burden was heavy. In prayer, I had the strangest feeling that came over me. I was almost too embarrassed to say anything but I could not take it any longer, I had to say something. I said, "I know this sounds strange because there is no way to confirm what I am sensing in my spirit but I come against the spirit of suicide! O God, please deliver this person from suicide!" I began to pray out loud against the spirit of suicide in the name of Jesus and when I prayed, Michelle said, "That's it Randy, that's it!"

God moved in a mighty way in that prayer. I felt kind of stupid because I did not know anyone there and there was no way I knew if what I was praying was real or not. All I could do is believe that God was leading. After prayer the burden had lifted and I actually could look out the window and not get sick.

As we talked about that prayer, I told Stephen and Michelle, I believed God showed me two things while I was praying. 1) The person was a male and 2) the person was or was going to be lonely and he could not handle that.

I have to be honest here and say a part of me felt like a fool. There was no way to confirm what I believed in my spirit. Before I left the room, I added, "Jesus, would you please show us that you lead us here without a doubt? Will you show us that I have not lost my mind and that you really did want me to pray that prayer?" Again, little did I know God was teaching me obedience.

The next day, Stephen and Michelle were on the beach. While they laid there next to people Stephen overheard a conversation between two girls. The conversation was about one of the girls and her boyfriend that she had just broken up with. Apparently, the young man was devastated over that. One of the girls said, "I was concerned about him and went out to see if he was ok and he was on the balcony getting ready to jump but he finally

came to his senses and got down."

Thank God for his mercy on that young man!

Chapter 10   A Man Claimed For Jesus

On June 12, 1998, I was on patrol on one of the back roads of Anderson County. It was a very narrow road. All of a sudden around a curve at a high rate of speed was a white van and it was heading straight for me. I had no place to go because there were embankments and woods on both sides of me. I drove into the embankment as much as I could to get away from the speeding van.

Somehow (by God's grace) the van managed to squeeze in between my cruiser and the embankment on the other side of the road without hitting anything. I couldn't believe the van missed me.

I turned the cruiser around as fast as I could so I could catch up to the van. Thankfully, instead of continuing on speeding away the driver of the van tried to "out fox" me and drove up a gravel driveway several hundred feet away.

I radioed dispatch and asked for back-up but my nearest back-up was about 30 minutes away. Instead of waiting for back-up I approached the van and made the driver get out. Immediately I smelled alcohol and he was obviously intoxicated.

I arrested the driver and called for a wrecker. It took the wrecker over an hour to get there on the scene.

During this hour the man began talking with me and gave me his name. He began telling me how he knew there was a God and that he believed in him but things in his life were just not right. He admitted and said that he was "running" from God.

I shared with this man and told him that I was thankful that neither one of us were hurt or killed, and that I would be praying for him and that many people have made mistakes throughout their life. It isn't the mistakes that define people but what they do with those mistakes and about them.

A few nights later I was in church. After service a good friend of mine walked up to me. Joe Tackett walked up and said he appreciated what I did for his brother. I didn't know what he was talking about so I asked him to clarify what he meant. He then explained to me that the man I arrested a few days prior was his brother, Chris Tackett. I had no idea it was his brother. I never made the connection with the two last names.

Joe told me that he was thankful that it was me who had arrested Chris and not someone else. He stated the incident really shook Chris up and he was hoping that this may be a "turning point" for him.

I told Joe that I would certainly be praying for Chris over the next several months. Word finally came....

Chris Tackett gave his heart and life to Jesus and he was off the drugs and alcohol.

Now, I've been a police officer a long time. I know how people can get "Jailhouse Religion". People often use God to get out of trouble then later go right back to where they were.

This was not going to be Chris' story.

A few years had passed and I had lost contact with Chris and even Joe at this point. I had not seen Chris since our last day in court five years before.

In September of 2003, I was at an event called, "Worship In The Park" in Oak Ridge, TN. While I was talking with some friends and family, I noticed this man walking up to me. The man had a glow on his face and you could tell he had Jesus all in him as his smile was from ear to ear.

It was Chris Tackett. I did not recognize it was him until he told me. I was amazed. He looked amazing.

Chris began to thank me for the day we met. We both hugged each other and rejoiced and thanked God for what He had done. Chris then told me that he is now a Youth Pastor and that God was still moving in his life.

I was able to introduce Chris to my parents who were visiting from WV. I told them that I could not remember the date when we met but it had been a few years ago. Chris spoke up with a smile on his face and said, "Oh I didn't forget. It was June 12th! I'll never forget that day."

As of this writing, I am extremely thrilled to tell you that Chris did not just get "Jailhouse Religion". He got the real deal. He is still on fire for God and is still a Youth Pastor.

What an amazing God we serve.

Chapter 11 The Man In The Green Shirt

On April 28, 2001, on a Saturday morning the Holy Spirit woke me up around 8:00am. He said, "Go tell the man in the green shirt that I love him."

I thought that was a funny thing so I turned back over and tried to go back to sleep. Again in my spirit I heard it but I just ignored it because I thought it was all in my mind.

A third time it happened but this time I literally felt someone beside me and hands were on my shoulder pushing on me to wake up. It felt so real that I remember turning back over to look to see who was there but there wasn't anyone. Again I heard in my spirit, "I said, 'Go tell the man in the green shirt that I love him!'"

Reluctantly I got up and I put my clothes on and headed out the door and drove toward the bank. I remember feeling so stupid. I was thinking that I really lost it this time.

I also remember as I crossed over the Weaver Bridge in Clinton, that God must have a sense of humor and that there was probably a bowling team on the parking lot of the bank and they were all dressed in green uniform shirts. But as I pulled on the parking lot of the bank I noticed there was no bowling team. In fact, I don't even remember seeing any vehicles on the lot. But, I parked my vehicle and walked into the bank anyway.

When I walked in, there was no one inside the lobby of the bank and no one in line waiting to be waited on. As I quickly scanned the teller line I saw three female tellers and at the end (actually at the beginning of the line) was one sole man being waited on and he was wearing a green shirt.

My heart almost came to a stop. I quickly turned around and walked right straight out the door. My heart was in my throat and I remember as I paced the sidewalk I began to panic and was thinking, "What am I going to do? What am I going to say?" and the Holy Spirit again said, "Tell the man in the green shirt that I love him."

As the man came out of the door I interrupted him and said, "Sir, may I speak to you?" (Thousands of thoughts running through my head like, 'I do not know this man!', 'He's going to think I'm nuts!!', and this one.....He probably thinks I'm going to rob him.')

But I said, "Sir, may I speak to you?"

He said, "Yes."

I said, "I know you don't know me but the Holy Spirit woke me up this morning and told me to come here and tell the man in the green shirt that He loves him. So, Sir, Jesus loves you!"

This man bowed his head and with tears in his eyes he said, "I used to preach!" He continued and said, "Sir, do you know why I am here?" I said, "No, sir."

He said, "I am here because I've turned my back on God, left the church and started my own business. I am here because I am taking the last money we have to go buy food for the family and pay on the rest of the bills."

Right then the Holy Spirit welled up inside of me and I began to exhort and encourage this man. I told him that if he would repent and ask God to forgive him and do what God had planned for him to do then God would see his every need met.

I asked the man if I could pray for him and he said that I could.

After I prayed for the man, we shook hands and he told me his name is Alan Giles. I told him my name and gave him a card with my name on it and then we departed.

Three weeks later Alan called me and told me that God had forgiven him and he once again is preaching the Gospel of Jesus Christ. Praise The Lord!

Ten years later I learned that Pastor Alan Giles is still a pastor and is still on fire for God. In fact it's my understanding that he is the Senior Pastor at one of the largest churches in Anderson County.

I am thankful for God's mercy and divine order. I am thankful that God knows my heart and knows that even though I may be slow to obey, He knows that I will obey Him no matter what it is. God will give you the same type of leadings if you will only spend time with Him, walk with Him and follow Him. This is our calling.

I give God all the glory and all the honor for His grace is truly sufficient!!!

Chapter 12   **The Branson Trip**

(A Modern Day Bible Story)

On July 8, 2001, I woke up around 7:00am. When I did I heard in my heart, "Branson, Missouri!" That's all I heard and that's all that was said, nothing else. I thought that was very weird and asked God what He meant by that but He said nothing else. My brother-n-law and my sister were in WV because my brother-n-law had to preach in Morgantown. Later that evening my wife, Lisa and I were at their residence with our kids. My brother-n-law came down the steps and told me that while he was in WV God told him that he and I were "...taking a trip." He said, "I don't know where we are going but I know that you and I are going somewhere." I started laughing and said, "I know where."

I told him what had happened to me that morning. We sat down outside on the patio and began to talk and try to figure out what God was trying to tell us. My brother-n-law said that he felt there was a person that we needed to minister to.

As we talked, we felt the presence of God around us and we knew we were not to tell anyone about our trip. My brother-n-law said, "I feel that we are to leave on September 28th and return the 30th" for wherever we are going. I said, "I think that the trip we're supposed to take is on a weekend. It will be interesting to see what the dates you said are on."

We immediately got up and went inside his place and looked at a calendar. Wouldn't you know it? September 28, 29 and 30th were on a weekend. I said, "Well the only thing that will settle it for me now and convince me that God is trying to tell us something, is if I am scheduled off that weekend." (As you know, most police officers work a lot of crazy shifts.)

Again looking at the calendar I figured out my schedule and to our amazement I was scheduled off for that weekend. God confirmed that He really was talking to us and we were to go to Branson, Missouri. We began to laugh and we both became very excited. I said, "I know now that we are to go to Branson, Missouri". But there was a problem. Neither one of us knew anyone in Branson.

One night in late July or early August I was at my brother-n-law's house and again we were talking about the trip. During our talk it was again said that we were going to minister to one person. Right then God showed me a vision of a man in a dark corner with a white shirt and blue jeans on and he had dark hair. The man was very discouraged and torn within himself. I felt hopelessness in my heart. It was like the man in the vision was ready to give up and quit. This was so vivid that I knew I needed to write it down. Another thing we said was that we were not to buy the plane tickets until the first week in September.

As the weeks passed we remained in prayer about the trip. Soon it was time to get the plane tickets. We knew we shouldn't pay more than $100 to $150 a ticket. I felt $100 but my brother-n-law felt no more than $150. We also felt that we were to leave in the morning and arrive back home in the evening.

I called the airlines directly to price the plane tickets. All tickets were priced from $250 to $1,040 a ticket. We thought about going through Priceline.com but the problem with that was you cannot choose your times of flights. You have to take what they give you and you cannot change it once they do give it to you. So now we were on "trust" street.

After we prayed about it there was nothing else for us to do except trust God. We knew He was leading us so we had to trust Him to get us the right times we needed. I ordered our tickets through priceline.com trusting Jesus to help.

After I placed the bid for $100 it was accepted. By the time we paid fees for this and that our tickets were $149 and some change for each.

And the times of the flights? The flight out was scheduled in the morning and the return flight was scheduled in the evening. WHAT A MIGHTY GOD WE SERVE!!!!

Lisa and my sister were asking us about the trip. They were wondering what in the world we were up to because they knew we were planning something. We told them that God was leading us to Missouri. It was completely a leap of faith and no one knew we were coming because we didn't know anyone to meet.

We had never been there before. We had no hotel reservations, no car rental and only a little amount of money. The only thing I knew was that I was to take my singing tapes and some books called, *A VOICE IN THE WILDERNESS* by Loran W. Helm.

My wife said, "You mean to tell me that you are going to Branson, MO and you don't know anyone there, you don't know who you are going to see, no one knows you're coming, you have no hotel room to stay in, you have no car rental and you have little to no money?" I said, "Yeah, that's what I'm telling you." Lisa and my sister thought we were crazy.

Then on September 11, 2001, the terrorists attacked in New York and in Washington, DC. All flights everywhere were cancelled. We had already bought our tickets and now we could not get our money back. We had to take the trip. Again, our wives thought we were nuts.

The week we were to leave on our flight, I felt that we needed to leave even earlier than our 10:45am scheduled flight. I didn't know how to do this because priceline.com could not change our flight times and now with the new security at the airports, I did not think they would let us do it anyway.

Even after prayer, that feeling would not leave me. So, on the morning of our flight we got up at 4:00am because there was an early flight at 6:20am. I thought that maybe we could go and be put on a standby list. When we got to the airport, Lisa dropped us off and left because she couldn't go in the gates because of the new security.

After we got up to the counter the lady told us that she couldn't change our flights. She could not even put us on standby. This meant that we now had to wait until 10:45 for our flight. Then she said that she would change it this one time but that our flight out of St. Louis could not be changed. She asked us to put our luggage on the table so they could be searched. When she opened my luggage she saw my Bible and said, "That's a good book to have." She finished searching my case and then went to my brother-n-law.

He had a Bible and a few of Rev Helm's books. She said, "What is this, a church trip?" I said, "No Ma'am, this is a

God trip. We feel that God has lead us to go to Missouri."
She did not say another word. She finished searching the
luggage and went back to the counter. Without saying a
word to us she not only put us on the next flight out of
Knoxville but also had us on the next flight out of St. Louis.
Praise the Lord!

We landed in Springfield, MO and got a rental car and
drove to Branson. While we were enroute to Branson my
brother-n-law said, "When we can, we need to find a
phone book and look through it."

When we arrived in Branson we pulled off the exit and
noticed this big Baptist Church. Something about it
touched our hearts but we did not know what it was. So we
first drove through town and began looking for a hotel or
motel to stay in. Out of the many hotels there were three
hotels that caught our eye.

We stopped into the first one but I could sense that it was not the one we were to stay at. So we drove around more. My brother-n-law saw a hotel and said he felt impressed to stop. When we stopped in we asked the clerk about their room rate. It was too much for us.

Before we left she began to talk about "Lower Branson" and pointed to it on a local map with her finger. While she was talking, it was like bombs going off in my heart. It was like my heart was doing flips. As we walked out of the door I said, "My heart is going crazy". I never felt it like that before. I said, "We have to go to Lower Branson..."

We drove on to the lower part of Branson. When we were there we could sense God's presence strongly but we could not understand what He was trying to tell us. We drove around but we couldn't locate anything. It was as if there was a blockage or something so we drove back up the hill to where the hotels were.

After prayer we felt that God lead us to a hotel. Later that evening we were inside our room and my brother-n-law got a phone book and began looking through it. Without saying anything he put it down.

I then picked up the phone book and began looking through it. There were ten yellow pages of churches and between 1,400 to 1,600 names on those pages. When I got to a certain pastors name it was like it jumped off the page at me. The name was Rev. Jim Cariker.

I said, "I am going to call the number". My brother-n-law said, "What are you going to say to them?" I said, "I don't know." Somehow, God gave me strength to call the phone number.

A female answered the phone. It was Gloria Cariker. I asked to speak to Pastor Cariker. She said he wasn't home but could take a message. I said, "Well, you don't know me but my name is Randy Myers. My brother-n-law and I are here in Branson because we felt that Jesus sent us here on a mission.

She was kind and began to talk to me. During the talk I said, "Ma'am, has your husband been discouraged?" She said, "He sure has!" She began to talk as though she knew who I was. In the conversation I found out that he is a pastor of a Nazarene Church.

I thought that was interesting because I was raised in a Nazarene Church as a child. Then Ms. Cariker invited us to her church on Sunday and said, "…and maybe you can sing for us."

Now, how did she know I sang and brought my tapes? I told her nothing of that. I said, "Well, you won't believe this but I do sing and I did bring a few tapes." About that time her husband walks into the house.

Pastor Cariker gets on the phone and I requested to meet him on Saturday morning. He agreed to meet us and began to tell us where his church was. Guess where it is located? **LOWER BRANSON**!! We had drove right passed the street earlier in the day that took us there. By this time we are pumped. We were so excited and yet scared. What were we going to say to this man? We didn't even know him.

We were so excited that we had to go see where the church was located. We drove back down to lower Branson at night and found the church. It was located in a dark corner. I saw only one street light around the whole area and it was covered by tree branches and leaves.

The next morning we got up and prayed before we left. In my prayer God gave me another vision. I saw a Shepherd standing in the field with a staff but there were very few sheep standing around him. During this vision God said,

"Read 2nd Chronicles 7:12." God was telling me to tell this man He hears his prayers.

Leaving to meet this man at his church, Branson Nazarene, my brother-n-law said, "Now if this man has dark hair, I am going to go nuts. If he doesn't, I'm leaving."

When we arrived, the church door was open so we went on in. When the Pastor came out of his office, we couldn't believe our eyes. Exactly as I saw in my vision, the pastor had dark hair and he was wearing a white shirt and blue jeans.

We introduced ourselves and the pastor invited us to sit down. He began telling us that he only had ten minutes to give us. My brother-n-law said, "That's fine we are only here to encourage you Jesus told us to come here."

We shared this story with him and told him about my vision with him in jeans and a white shirt. He laughed and said that he had been the pastor of that church for nineteen years and he never wore jeans to the office.

He then began to pour his heart out to us. He told us that he was in a place just a few weeks ago and was almost "…ready to throw in the towel." If you could have heard this man's story you would have been amazed to see how God helped him to hang on and not quit.

He told us of how he was losing all of his people to other things. Key people in his church were leaving him to go do their ministry in other places. A Shepherd was losing his sheep. He said that a man of God had told him three years ago that, "God was going to prune his church". As he shared you could see the tears in Pastor Cariker's eyes. He smiled and said, "But I didn't think he meant the whole church."

"September 11th was probably the hardest day…" He said. Not only because of the terrorist attacks but because that was the day one of his deacons came and told him he was leaving the church. This man had been with him for a long time.

After about an hour we left Pastor Cariker's office. It wasn't because we over stayed, but was because this man poured his heart out and all we did was listen. As he shared, God reminded me of 2nd Chronicles 7:12. With as much love as I could show I told the pastor that God revealed to me in prayer what he was going through and that God had said, "He has heard your prayers". Needless to say, by the time we left, Pastor Cariker was encouraged.

What an awesome meeting it was. Hallelujah! God is amazing! It is amazing how He can use two willing servants if we would just be willing to obey. You could just feel the love that Pastor Cariker had in his heart.

On Sunday morning we arrived at the church. As we arrived there was also a bus full of people who were from

Spokane, WA. Pastor Cariker had such a light on his face. He introduced us to his church and told them the story of what had happened. Then he asked my brother-n-law to share and he asked me to sing.

Pastor Cariker then said, "I have already thanked these two men for their obedience but I want to tell them again publicly and before this church congregation that I accept their encouragement because it was truly of God."

Then Pastor Cariker began to preach in Genesis 12:1. It says, "The Lord said unto Abram, 'Leave your country, your people and your father's house and go to the land I will show you.'" Verse 4 says, "So Abram left as the Lord told him..."

Pastor Cariker reminded the people that God promised Abram nothing. He only told him to leave. And Abraham was obedient to God and it cost him to be obedient. He began to share what it really cost to obey Christ. It cost money and time, time away from your family. Sometimes there are misunderstandings and misinterpretations. People may think you're crazy. (That sounded familiar.) We just looked at each other and laughed.

Pastor Cariker continued that in the insurance business there are stress rating systems and in our lives there are life changing events. How much of these take a toll on our body? Abram did what God told him to do. But it came with a price.

My brother-n-law and I were in awe of the message. We were two men who just lived the very message that he was preaching. It was a confirmation to us that we were well in God's plan and His timing.

After church service, a lady came up to my brother-n-law and told him that before church service she had made up her mind this service would be the last church service that she would ever attend because she was so discouraged of

"Christians". But she said because of the story she heard that day and because of the obedience of two men, her faith was renewed. Praise The Lord!

God is so good and I love Him so much. Praise The Lord!

****

Here is an e-mail that Pastor Cariker sent on October 1, 2001, in response to our trip.

Pastor:

It was a real joy to get acquainted with you and Randy this weekend. I believe your visit was indeed ordered of the Lord! Not only were Gloria and I encouraged, but also our congregation was encouraged.

Thank you for sharing your words of encouragement with our church Sunday morning and for Randy's song. I appreciated your words of encouragement, hope & faith in Jesus as well as your sense of time constraints, and your humble spirit. I had several people asking about the details of our visit after church Sunday morning and again Sunday evening.

All I can say is that the presence of the Lord around those two men was stronger than I had ever felt before. My son and daughter were also touched by this. My son remarked that he still can't believe that God would send two men that we've never met all the way here to tell us that God loves us. If more of us could live by faith and obedience that which you & Randy have displayed this would definitely be a different place to live.

Thank you for being obedient to the Holy Spirit. I pray that your ministries will also be blessed of the Lord. I feel that the Lord has a wonderful church ministry waiting for you somewhere, and with your faith displayed here that ministry will truly be blessed.

In Christ,

Pastor Jim Cariker

Chapter 13　**My Calling**

I am so thankful to be used of God in such a way that only God could do. The Branson Trip story was truly a "modern day bible story" in my eyes, but the next four years after that trip I would be in a desert that seemed like would never end. For the next four years I would not hear God's voice at all. I became lonely, irritable and a miserable soul.

It became so bad that I doubted I was even a Christian. People would ask me to pray with them about things and it was almost as if God turned His nose up at me or turned His back on me.

I could not see God's hand in my life, could not hear His voice, nor could I sense His presence in my life. I did not even know if He was still with me or not. I was in a wilderness so deep that all I could do was keep walking and do what I knew was right. I felt lost.

In 2005, my brother-n-law and I made the trip back to Branson for a second time. Pastor Cariker was still going strong.

The ironic thing about the trip was on the way back, I heard the Holy Spirit speak to me again for the first time in four years. As our plane took off from Springfield, MO I heard the Holy Spirit say, "Get your Bible and read Ezekiel chapter 2 and chapter 3."

When I heard that I was very excited. I wanted to get my Bible and do as He said, but the "Fasten Seatbelt" sign was still on and the plane still climbing. I knew I shouldn't get up.

Again, the Holy Spirit said, "Get your Bible and read Ezekiel chapter 2 and chapter 3." I unlatched my seatbelt, got up and opened the cupboard above me. As soon as my hand touched the Bible the Holy Spirit spoke again and said, "Read Ezekiel chapter 2 and chapter 3". Sitting down I heard Him say, "This is your calling."

I was thrilled because I always wanted to know what my calling was. As I read the Bible I could feel the anointing. I began to cry as the call of God was falling on me there on that plane. The Word I read was very sobering and shook me to my core.

I knew my calling was to the Church. Not just a church but to God's Church. Not just to those who attend church but to those whom God has called into His Kingdom. Far too long there have been "men of God" who have preached things that have not completely lined up with God's Word; things that have been taken out of context or misrepresented. I've heard preachers preach things that have basically given people a "license" to sin. But God's Word teaches us that we are to be holy and blameless and He has instructed me to share that word and remind us all, that He is coming for a pure and holy Church. If I do not share this word then there are those whose blood will be on my hands. That's a risk I cannot take.

God has given me the burden to share His Truth to all who will listen, and I will say upfront that I, like Paul, do not count myself to have apprehended this walk completely but I too am pressing on for the prize of the high calling of Jesus Christ. I admittedly still struggle with things today but with God as my Helper and Strength, I will overcome.

A short time later the Holy Spirit showed me I was to hold revival in Elkview, WV. In July of 2005, God helped me to preach three nights. People were being helped and you could feel the anointing in the building but I believe it was the last night of the revival that Jesus showed up in power.

During the message that night I was preaching and I can remember saying, "What does God have to do to prove to us that He is returning?" All of a sudden there was thunder that was deep, long and then became very loud. The thunder was so strong it literally shook the building. Trust me when I say it got people's attention.

As I was trying to close out service, I remember saying "Wasn't it crazy when the thunder hit as I said, 'What does God have to do.....' I couldn't even finish that sentence when all of sudden the fire alarm began to sound and all of the lights in the auditorium began to flash on and off for about 10 seconds. The amazing thing is the fire department never showed up to check on the building.

I think God was trying to tell us something. Needless to say there was a great alter call that night. If I remember correctly there were about sixteen souls saved.

Thank you, Jesus.

Chapter 14 **A Ministry Born**

International C.O.P.S. Ministries
"Citizens Obediently Praying for Safety"

As I said earlier, throughout 1997, I felt like God was trying to tell me to start a ministry for police officers. I didn't really know what to do or how to start it. I remember talking to one of my partners and telling him about it and what I was thinking. He said he liked the concept. However, something happened and I never pursued it after that until the Fall of 2003, when I kept looking back over my career and seeing God's hand on me and even sparing my life because I had someone praying for me by name.

This was the time in my life that I wasn't hearing from God. I did not know for sure if God would be pleased with this or not but I know He spoke to me in 1997. At this time in my life I only knew to do the things I was previously told..... What I believed in. (When you do not know what to do, just do and keep doing the things you were told.)

I called a good friend who was a long time friend, Stephen Carpenter and he helped me get the ministry up and running. Stephen is an attorney and owns his own law firm so he was able to do all the legal work for me.

Over the next year I began to promote the ministry and encouraged police officers, correctional officers and 911 dispatchers to sign up and allow us to pray for them by name on a daily basis. I know it's bribery but officers LOVE free stuff so I told all officers that if they would sign up I would give them a free t-shirt from the C.O.P.S. Ministry. It was working.

I was asked about a logo to be put on our web page. Sgt J. N. of Knox County Sheriff's Officer was going to be our web master and wanted to put it on the site. I told him we did not have a logo yet but it was ok for now. I told him I could not explain what it looked like in my mind but I would know it when I saw it.

In four years time we had 58 officers in three counties. I was working hard by myself to get the ministry up and running but I still did not have a logo.

In 2005, our ministry was able to give every police officer, correctional officer and 911 dispatcher a Bible. We gave out close to 300 Bibles county-wide.

In mid May to early June of 2007, the Holy Spirit began talking to me about the ministry. He asked me, "Son, are you going to do this ministry or not?" I answered and said, "God, I am doing this ministry." He never said anything else so I continued with my business at hand.

Several days later the Holy Spirit came to me again the second time and said, "Son, are you going to do this ministry or not?" I thought that was strange but again I answered, "I am doing this ministry."

Yet several days later once again the Holy Spirit came to me for the third time and said, "Son, are you going to do this ministry or not?" By this time I was frustrated. I said, "God I am doing this ministry. Don't you remember in 2005 we gave every officer in Anderson County a Bible?" (As if He didn't already know that)

My mind began to take over all my thoughts. I started looking at everything I was doing. At the time, I had three children playing basketball in a league. I myself was the Co-Director of the basketball program and I was coaching two different teams. On top of that, I was also on the praise team at the church and working full time.

I said, "Ok, God. I quit everything! I quit everything except the C.O.P.S. Ministry. Is this what you're telling me to do? I surrender ALL to You. I'll do whatever you want me to do."

I heard nothing but I resigned from everything I was in. I quit the basketball program, I stopped coaching the two teams and I stepped down from the Praise Team at church. People thought I was mad and wondered what in the world I was doing. I tried to assure them I was not mad at anything or anyone, I just had to obey God and do what I thought was right for that time.

Within days of surrendering all and making the decision to obey and resign everything, Daniel and I were at a store on Edgemoor Road. As we began to back out of a parking spot I saw a lady driving a car and it had a license plate on the front that said, "COPS" and it was in blue letters. The car pulled into a parking spot beside us.

I pulled back into the parking spot I was in. Daniel asked what I was doing and I told him what I saw. I told him I was going to ask the lady what the sign was.

As I got out of the car, I said, "Excuse me, but what is your front license plate about." This kind lady told me about an organization called, "Concerns of Police Survivors" and stated she became a member of that organization when her former brother-n-law was killed in Knox County. She stated that the organization helps families in their time of need after an officer is killed in the line of duty.

I had never heard of this group before. I then told this lady that I too use the acronym C.O.P.S. for the ministry I have and that our C.O.P.S. stands for "Citizens Obediently Praying for Safety". Obviously, she had never heard of us since we had not been doing it for long.

She told me her name is Donna Lyon Barker and stated she wanted to get involved with our ministry if I had room. As it turned out Donna ended up being the first member of our staff and is still with me today.

That weekend I went to a church in Knoxville that I had never been to before. As I sat there, a man walked up to me and placed his Bible in front of me. He said he felt like the Holy Spirit told him to show me a passage and wanted me to read it.

I don't remember the passage but I remember what it meant to me. As I read that passage, God was telling me that if I would obey Him and do what He asked me to do He would be with me and help me.

After church, I walked up to this man and thanked him for his obedience and told him the passage helped. We then introduced ourselves. The man said his name is Mark Ortiz.

That night I had a C.O.P.S. Ministry polo shirt on. Mark saw the polo shirt and asked me what it was. I began to tell him about our ministry. As I told him, he had a certain curious look on his face then said, "I have something I'd like for you to see but I have to e-mail it to you." I said, "Ok" and gave him my e-mail address.

A couple of days passed and I got an e-mail from Mark. It was a copy of a hand sketched drawing. I could not believe my eyes, it was so amazing.

I replied to the e-mail and said, "Mark, I knew you were not expecting this. Quite frankly, neither was I. But may we please have this drawing for our logo? I believe this logo is for our ministry for the following reasons.

1) It looks like a shield and this ministry is for police officers

2) There are angels on both sides of the shield and their back is to the shield which means they are protecting the shield. Our ministry is called, "Citizens Obediently Praying for Safety" and I feel like the angels are a representation of the families who are praying for the officers.

3) There's a cross on it which is obviously a Christian symbol

4) The cross has a dove on it. It's a "Dove / Cross" combination with the sun in the back ground. In every "Dove / Cross" combination I've ever seen the dove is usually descending. But I find it interesting that in this combination the dove is ascending. I felt as if the Holy Spirit was saying to me that He is leading officers to the sun but not the s-u-n but to the S-O-N

5) The sun behind the mountain has rays shining down. I felt like the Holy Spirit was telling me that God is shining down on this ministry and that He approves of it.

6) I see the mountain behind the cross. I feel like that mountain was a representation of a police officer's life. Officer's lives are uphill battles with little down time.

7) As I looked at the drawing I then notice the ribbon at the bottom and how the ribbon at the bottom of the cross extended out past and around the shield. I felt like the Holy Spirit was telling me the ribbon is

a symbol of God's love for the officers and that at the times of their weakness He was binding their knees to the cross.

"So may we PLEASE have this drawing for our logo?" As I sent the e-mail reply back the Holy Spirit told me I forgot something. I thought to myself, "You just gave me one of the greatest revelations of my life. What in the world did I forget?"

The Holy Spirit told me to look again at the dove. I then noticed an olive branch in his mouth and the Holy Spirit asked me, "What does the olive branch represent?" I immediately said, "Peace" and then I realized that Police Officers are sometimes called, "Peace Officers".

Wow! What a revelation this was! I could not believe what I was seeing. I sent Mark the e-mail and waited for his response.

Mark and I then met one day and talked about my request. He told me the story about how this drawing came to be. He said that he drew the picture in 1997 (Remember? This was the exact same year that God birthed this ministry in my heart!) He and his wife lived in Denver, CO at the time and the Holy Spirit woke him up and told him to draw a picture. He said years later they moved to Oak Ridge, TN, (Can you believe that?) and that he lost the drawing in the move. He then stated that one week before he met me he found the drawing.

WOW! One week before he met me? That was the same week I resigned from all of the extra activities I was in. Can you believe that? God was working on others the same time He was working on me.

Mark continued to tell me that he was going to give this drawing to the ministry. He said the Holy Spirit had told him at the time of this drawing that this drawing would go around the world. He said, "I'm going to give you this drawing but you have to understand this logo is going International. Are you ready for that?" I told him by God's grace, I was.

What I'm about to tell you is nothing short of a miracle.

From June of 2007 to March of 2008, the ministry exploded and our numbers went from one state and 58 local officers to twenty-three states and over two hundred officers. I also obtained five people who said they wanted to be a part of the ministry and became volunteer staff members.

In May of 2008, our ministry was featured on "Live At Five" where a news reporter interviewed me and did a four minute segment on the ministry.

From March to October 2008, the ministry doubled again and then we went from twenty-three states to thirty states. C.O.P.S. Ministry went from over two hundred officers to over four hundred officers and we had five staff members. Our volunteers also grew from zero to around twenty.

I couldn't believe what God was doing. One Saturday we had a pancake breakfast to honor all law enforcement personnel. The event started at 8am. At 7:45am there was a lady approaching the door so I opened it for her and smiled and began to tell her that we would open up in fifteen minutes. She smiled and said, "I'm not here to eat, I'm here to volunteer." I had never met her before in my life but God put it on her heart to join this ministry.

Also in 2008, I was interviewed on a national radio show and was selected as their "Hero of the day". The radio show is called, "Seize the Day" with Gus Lloyd. A Police Officer in Massachusetts wrote Gus and nominated me for the honor of "Hero of the day" and told his story of being protected and of our ministry.

This police officer's name is Officer Matt S. (He asked that we not use his last name). Matt told me and the radio show that he had signed up with our ministry and that he was thankful for the family praying for him. He stated the prayers worked one day as he was responding to a call. With the lights and siren on, Officer S. was going through an intersection and was "T-boned" in his driver's side door. Officer S. stated he was able to walk away from the accident unhurt and he contributed that miracle to the prayers of the family that was praying for him.

In January 2009, our ministry went International and became "International C.O.P.S. Ministries".

I was on duty one day when I received a phone call in the middle of conducting a traffic stop. As I sat back down in the cruiser to run a drivers status, my cell phone rang and a very strange phone number appeared on the screen. This number literally had about 15 numbers going across.

I know I shouldn't have but my curiosity got the best of me so I answered the phone. The voice on the other end said, "Hello from across the pond." This voice had and an extreme English accent and rightfully so because they were calling me from England. I couldn't believe what I was hearing. I didn't want to be rude to the caller but I asked her to call me back in five minutes. I then let the driver go and waited anxiously for the second call.

This lady called me back for the second time. She stated she found our ministry web site on the internet and wanted to sign up as a pray-er. I told her that she was the first person from out of this country to sign up with our ministry, so I wanted to send her some items just for signing up.

As it turns out this world really is a "small world after all". As we talked I learned that I actually worked with her daughter in one of the agencies I used to work for.

In 2011, our ministry had continued to grow. We were now in 6 countries and had over eight hundred law enforcement personnel and four state chapters.

Today our ministry is in eight countries (USA, England, Canada, South Africa, Israel, Italy, Netherlands and Belgium), we have volunteers in six different states (OH, MO, WA, GA, FL and TX) who help promote the ministry in their state. We also have law enforcement personnel represented in thirty-five states in the U.S. and we have given away almost one thousand t-shirts to law enforcement personnel. We also have eight staff members and access to many local volunteers.

Every year this ministry receives stories throughout the country about how God has spared the lives of officers who are on our list. Officers in Florida that were shot but live today because of prayer. A Trooper in AZ stated he fell asleep at the wheel and is alive after he wrecked his cruiser on the interstate just missing five cars, and so on.

Throughout the years of this ministry, I have received e-mails from police officers who were contemplating suicide. One of those e-mails came in December 2007, from a police officer in West Virginia.

Officer Eric S. wrote me and asked, "Do you believe God allows people into heaven no matter how they get there?" He shared his story about how his wife left him after several years of marriage. He said he didn't really want to end his life and you could feel his pain in this e-mail. He told me he did not mind sharing his story with me because he knew it was covered under the confession to a religious official. Then he jokingly said, "Plus you don't know where I'm from in case (the above) doesn't work." (Even in distress and peril officers try their best to find humor in a situation.)

I immediately replied to the e-mail and begged this officer to call me as soon as he could. Amazingly, he called me. After ministering to him a while on the phone I asked him how he found out about the ministry. He said that he was "surfing the net" and found our web site. I was amazed to learn that this officer was actually a police officer in the city I grew up in. (Can you imagine that? Of all the ministries in the world he found our ministry on the website he and contacted me!)

Several weeks went by and I would minister to this officer over the phone. After a series of phone calls, I was able to lead this police officer to Jesus. He prayed and asked Jesus to forgive him and come into his heart. Praise the Lord.

In September of 2012, I was in WV visiting my parents and attending a Ministers Conference at Maranatha Fellowship in Saint Albans, WV. I put on the internet that I was in town if anyone wanted to see me. Within minutes I was contacted by Officer S. who wanted to meet me. He said he had been waiting for the chance to meet me because there was something he wanted to share.

The next day I drove several miles away to meet this officer. When I met him he gave me a hug and had tears in his eyes. He said, "I am so thankful to meet you after all these years. I've wanted to tell you something I've never told anyone before." He said, "What you don't know is, I was so distressed I felt like a complete failure in life after losing my first wife. Before I called you I actually tried to kill myself. I placed the pistol in my mouth and pulled the trigger but the primer did not fire." As he wept with me on the sidewalk he said, "I remember being so mad at myself because I couldn't even kill myself right. But something made me get up. I got up and found your website on the internet. When I reached out to you I had no idea that you were from here. If you wouldn't have been there for me I know I would have tried to kill myself again."

Today, Officer Eric S. is doing very well. He has recovered from his depression and has since remarried and now has a set of twins with his new wife. Praise the Lord!

I want to share of another miracle story with you that happened to a good friend of mine. This story actually happened in Knoxville, TN.

Trooper Rusty C. was on duty and running radar on a two lane road. He observed a speeding car going in the opposite direction. As Trooper C. was making a U-Turn to go after the speeding vehicle he was "T-boned" in the driver's door. The accident was so severe that he was trapped in the vehicle and had to be cut out with the "Jaws-of-life". Rusty was flown to an area hospital with a broken pelvis and many other medical issues.

I received word of the incident but at the time I was not told it was Rusty. When I received the phone call of the incident I immediately sent out an emergency prayer chain message and asked people to pray for the injured Trooper. I did not receive Rusty's name until several days later. My heart sank.

Eventually, when I was able to speak to Rusty, he told me that the doctors had told him he would never work again or walk without a limp. But because of the prayers that were going up for him God had other plans. Within eight weeks Rusty was back up and on full duty.

I could tell you many stories of God's miracle hand in the lives of officers. I have several stories that involve me personally that I could share but for the sake of keeping this a "book" and not a novel I will refrain.

I would like to mention by name the current staff members who have helped me throughout the years and who continue to support this ministry. These great people have dedicated a lot of time and energy and even money to the success of this ministry.

The first one I want to mention is Stephen Carpenter. Stephen is an attorney who has worked countless hours to help us and he has done this from his heart waiving the thousands of dollars he could have charged us. I am eternally grateful to him for everything that he has done.

Retired Captain, Gerald "Jerry" King is retired from Knoxville Police Department. Jerry served as our Vice President for years and has recently stepped down from that title but still serves with us as a member of the International Board of Directors.

Corporal Rick Neace is currently employed with the Union City Police Department in Union, MO, and has graciously accepted the Vice President's role. Rick and his wife Kristi are extremely active in law enforcement ministry. Kristi travels the country talking to the spouses of officers and has written a few books along the way.

Deputy Scott Lucas is currently employed with the Anderson County Sheriff's Office and serves as our 2nd Vice President. Scott and I have been like brothers for almost thirty years now and his wife, Niki, is the Founder of the East Tennessee LEO Wives. Her ministry is a support group for wives whose husbands serve full time in law enforcement.

Donna Barker serves as our Secretary. Donna has been a great help to me in that role. Donna was married at one time to an officer and understands the life that officers live. Her former brother-n-law was killed in the line of duty several years ago so she also understands the pain associated with such a tragedy.

Julie Culver works for the Knox County Sheriff's Office and serves on the International Board of Directors. I cannot say enough about this lady. She has a heart of gold the size of Jupiter.

Julie is over our "Card Care" ministry and she has chosen to purchase these cards with her own money and mails out birthday cards every single day to every officer that has a birthday. Julie and I like to tease each other about who gives the most money to this ministry, me or her. I think she's won every year except one or two. She loves this ministry so much and I really do not know what I would do without her. (Lisa and I love you, Julie.)

Retired Sgt. Jim Neubert is retired from the Knox County Sheriff's Office. Jim is our web master and keeps our web page up and running. He is currently overseas on the mission field ministering the love of Jesus to souls in need.

As with any business or ministry the numbers of people involved fluctuate. There are so many people who have helped me with this ministry throughout the years that it would be close to impossible to name them all. But Kathy H. from Claxton, I say THANK YOU, for helping me in the very beginning and helping me keep things straight.

Many months throughout the year there is really not much to do but near the end of the year it gets really hard. Our volunteers have to review the list and make sure that officers are still with their agency.

When we were a "local" ministry it wasn't too bad. But now that we have over a thousand names on our lists the task is daunting. The turnover rate among law enforcement personnel is extremely high so it is very difficult to maintain an "up-to-date" list. Officers get fired, resign, retire or simply change agencies almost every day. The task is just as hard with the list of families that sign up to pray. Families move and forget to tell us so it's difficult to keep up with that list as well.

Thank you to each and every staff member and volunteer that is or has been with me. There is absolutely no way that I can do this ministry by myself and I sincerely thank each of you from the bottom of my heart. There will be souls in heaven because of your relentless efforts.

Chapter 15　**Not As It Appears**

Being obedient to the Holy Spirit has not always been an easy task for me and certainly not without a price. I haven't always made the right choices or decisions and my life hasn't always been one that has pleased God.

As many good stories I have to share, I have that many or more bad stories of my failures. Let me give you an example.

One day I was working day shift. I was in the office building and I was walking behind one of my Captains. Walking up a set of stairs, a burden hit my heart for this man and the Holy Spirit told me to pray for him. I thought that was weird so I just kept walking. The thought again came to me to pray for him but I never stopped him and asked him to pray.

A couple of days later the captain was working at his desk and fell over on his desk with a massive heart attack. He was dead before he even hit the desk.

For obvious reasons I don't like reviewing those memories. Trust me when I say they are embedded in my brain and are the reasons I am the way I am today. I'd like to say I've learned my lessons but I still make mistakes and don't do everything I should. (Typical man)

When it came to my personal life and my home life, my failures were not exempt.

Due to my job as a police officer it takes a lot of time away from the family. I work crazy hours and long shifts and spend a lot of time away from the family because of it. When the kids were small, my wife often said she felt like a single mom trying to raise three kids on her own. Many times she had to go to events without me which meant she was often disciplining the kids by herself.

When the kids got older and became teens and I was able to work a shift that I could actually be at home at decent hours, spend time with the family, it was almost as if my wife felt I did not have the right to correct the kids. That's when the real trouble began.

I'm sharing with you from my heart and confessing that we had some major struggles. Some people thought our life was perfect and that my wife and I had this great and wonderful marriage. I heard people actually say we had "the perfect marriage", but our closest friends new different.

Yes, we tried to live a Christian life our whole adult life. We tried to obey and do things right but because of the struggles things were NOT as they appeared.

For years, Lisa and I had a "difficult" marriage. We were and really still are total and complete opposites. Because we spent so much time apart we actually grew apart in more ways than one.

Sometimes I was a very hateful person to her. I didn't necessarily do it to be mean to her. It's just the way I was. I didn't think before I spoke a lot of times.

Lisa would do things I thought were wrong and being the cop that I am I had to "control" the situation. I would say things to her that hurt her. I did not know the things I said hurt her. I was not trying to hurt her.

Don't get me wrong. She wasn't doing real bad things like drugs or sleeping around or committing some huge horrible sin. She just had her ways of doing things in her life, since I wasn't around, that I didn't care for and because of that I treated her in ways I later learned made her feel less than dirt at times. Regardless of my real intensions, this is how I unknowingly made her feel.

That's not to say my wife was perfect and never did anything wrong. Trust me when I say there really were issues that needed to get worked out.

Again, using the kids as one example; as the kids were in their teens, she undermined my authority as a father. Looking back, I believe she felt that because I missed so much home time with the family, that I did not have the right to correct the kids. Unfortunately, she would let the kids do things after I would punish them and that really set me off. I felt betrayed and useless.

Then, it got to the point that Lisa stopped disciplining the kids altogether. She would complain to me about how the kids were treating her but yet she would not do anything about it herself.

There were times when the kids would sass Lisa and I would hear it. I would correct them more harshly trying to "make up" for Lisa's lack of discipline.

I was wrong in the manner in which I handled those types of things which only made the "issues" worse.

What we as men have to understand is that sometimes our re-actions are worse than our spouses actions or non-actions. We can make the situation better or worse simply by how we respond to any given situation.

As the years would go on the struggles would seem to increase. I remember one year our arguments were so bad and they seemed like they were never going to end. Every prayer I prayed seemed to only go to my nose and no higher. I couldn't see God's hand and I couldn't feel Him around me. I remember one time I called someone who was encouraging me to keep praying. I told him I couldn't pray and in fact I said, "My God isn't listening to me, so you tell **your** God I need some help down here!"

After years of constant turmoil and trouble in the home, Lisa kept threatening me with divorce. It got to the point that I could not take it anymore. I remember telling her the next time she threatened me with divorce that I would get the divorce and she would not have to worry about it. By this time our kids were grown. Daniel was in college and the girls were almost out of high school.

In May of 2010, Lisa's final threat was produced. I do not think she realized I was to the point that I meant what I said. When she threatened me with divorce again, I looked at her and said, "You got it."

The very next day, without saying another word to her, I went to an attorney in Clinton to file the divorce papers. When I got into that office I sat in a chair across from the attorney and he said, "I understand that you want to file for a divorce. Are you sure you want to do that?" I couldn't even answer him. I completely lost it and began to cry worse than I have ever cried before in my life. The pain in my heart was almost more than I could bear.

The attorney looked at me, leaned across his desk and said, "Breathe Randy, breathe!" I tried to regain my composure. He said, "Randy, you're not ready for this." I said, "I have to do this. More than anything I love my wife but more than that right now I just want the pain to stop. This is the only language she is going to understand."

Reluctantly, the attorney filled out the papers and the divorce papers were filed. I moved out of our house and moved to Lake City with some friends. Three days later there was a knock at the door. It was all three of our kids and they said, "Daddy, we're moving in with you."

When people began to learn of our separation they were shocked and couldn't believe their ears.

I had great friends that supported me. There were those that said, "Straighten up" and there were those that said, "Things are going to work out." There were those who simply said, "Man, whatever happens we're here for you."

My partners at work would check on me because they knew I was going through a rough time. There were two of them that went out of their way to be with me and tried to get my mind off of things. They took me and my girls out to dinner just to show their support at the most crucial time in our life. (J.T. and D.H. I still cannot thank you enough and I praise God for our friendship and what you mean to me.)

For the next week or more, there were six of us living in a two bedroom house. I gave the girls the spare bedroom, Daniel slept on the couch and I slept in the recliner.

The whole time the devil was putting in my head that Lisa did not love me and he told me she was cheating on me. I cannot describe to you the pain that was in my heart. At times I felt like I was dying.

After being gone for two weeks I felt like the Holy Spirit told me to, "get home now". It was the first time I heard Him speak to me in months. I suddenly picked up the bags and the kids and I went back home unannounced. Lisa had no idea I was coming.

When I got home there was no one there. Again, the devil would put thoughts in my head and accused my wife of doing things that simply were not true. The pain was more than I could take.

A few weeks had passed and the pain was still raw but even through this ordeal I still had to make myself continue to go to work.

One evening as I was driving to work, I was listening to the CD "Moving Forward" from Free Chapel. While listening, Jentezen Franklin was talking and all of sudden he said, "...your marriage shall NOT die but LIVE....." and when he said that I literally felt the power of God hit my heart. But I said, "NO!!! NO, Jesus!!

All I could think of at the time was the pain. I just wanted the pain to stop and was afraid that if I went back to the marriage it would just be the same thing all over again. I couldn't help but notice, however, that from that moment on God had given me a little glimmer of hope to hold on to.

I am truly thankful that He did not answer the spontaneous prayer that came out of my mouth.

What I did not know at that time was all those times the devil was telling me my wife was cheating on me she was actually going to see a marriage counselor. My wife had been going to counseling for a month without me. That was an amazing thing because we had tried counseling one other time before and it did not work. I begged my wife for years after that to go to counseling again with me but she refused to go. This time she went by herself.

She later told me she went for herself so she could learn and fix what she was doing wrong before we attempted to fix our problems as a couple. She had chosen to go see a Christian Counselor in Knoxville just off of Merchants Road.

One night Lisa came home and told me where she had been going and how the Counselor now wanted to speak with me. At first I was extremely angry that she would have even done that. I was angry because I felt she waited until AFTER I filed the divorce papers to even attempt to make me believe that she loved me and wanted things to work. For years I had felt like she didn't love me and now when I'm done with her she wanted to "try".

But, I went. I remembered the power in my heart a couple of days before and the small glimmer of hope God had given me in my heart.

Our marriage counselor was very tenderhearted, kind and compassionate. God used him to reach us and get us to do things that Lisa and I had not done in years. He got us to look at the other's side. (Believe it or not, men, our wives do have a point of view of things.)

The counselor began by sharing, 1 Peter 3:7. "Husbands, in the same way, live with your wives with an understanding of their weaker nature yet showing them honor as coheirs of the grace of life, so that your prayers will not be hindered." (HCSB)

Instantly I knew and understood why my prayers were not being heard. I learned that I had not been honoring my wife. I had not loved her and supported her in the way God had intended for me as a husband and my prayers were hindered because of it. Yes, Lisa may have been wrong in the things she did or said but I was also wrong and I was supposed to be the leader of the home and set the example.

I'm extremely happy and thrilled beyond measure to tell you that Lisa and I are still married today. We've been together now for 27 years and I must tell you the last three years have been greater than the first twenty-four years of marriage combined.

There is no way I could have ever made it through this ordeal without God and the help that I received from my close friends. From my people letting me move into their home, to my co-workers taking me out and calling me daily, to my life-long friend and brother who was there for me every day he could be. Every one of these people could have said, "Randy, just leave her...." But none of them ever did. They only said, "We're here for you." or "It's going to work out."

They only had positive things to say and I will be forever grateful for them and their friendship because now I truly have the love of my life and the woman of my dreams. My wife, Lisa, is just that.

There are friends and other people who have seen us in our time of struggles. They and even our kids have suffered greatly at the hands of two people who couldn't get a long for years but I'm here to tell you that God is a good God and He has restored our marriage! He is faithful.

Yes we have struggled many years. Yes, we have made some poor and bad decisions and said things we both regret but God has brought us through it. The difference maker was when we as a couple decided to walk in obedience to the Word of God. We had to surrender our wills and admit where we were wrong and then stop doing the things we were doing. It wasn't easy! We both had to deny our flesh and do what was right.

We both could have walked away. I'm sure most people closest to us thought maybe we should have. But there were no Biblical grounds for divorce on either side.

To my wife I say, Honey, thank you for choosing to stay with me. Thank you for not listening to the thoughts in your head and to friends and family who encouraged you to leave. You have become exactly what I have always believed you were deep down in your heart. AN AMAZING WOMAN! I am thankful that I am a changed man as well.

I love you with all of my heart and I look forward to being with you for the rest of my life.

Chapter 16   Final Word

I felt in my heart that I should encourage all of you who are reading this book.

Walking in obedience to the Holy Spirit is paramount. There are those who are waiting on you to be obedient. There are people whose lives you could be an encouragement to.

There are those of you who are struggling in your marriage and those of you who are struggling in your life in general. I'm here to tell you and to remind you that God knows exactly where you are and He loves you!

No matter what bad things you've done in your life, I want to encourage you and tell you to walk in obedience and surrender your life to Christ.

If you haven't already done so, PLEASE, surrender your life to Him. Give Him ALL of you and not just part of you. Don't just give Him you until He fixes whatever is wrong and then leave Him again. Be determined to follow Him, live with Him and have a relationship with Him forever.

The Bible says in John 15:19, "If you were of the world, the world would love you as its own. However, because you are not of the world, but I have chosen you out of it, the world hates you." (HCSB)

Did you catch that? "...but I have chosen you...." Even though you have failed, regardless of what that failure is, God Himself has chosen **YOU**!

Jesus did not choose you because He died on the cross for you; He died on the cross for you because He chose you. Even knowing you would do the things you've done, HE STILL chose you and He died on the cross for you.

Without God in our life we are nothing. Without Him leading us and guiding us we have nothing.

You may be like I was and keep making the same mistakes all the time. If you will spend time with Jesus, read the Bible, love Him and follow Him, I promise you that you will stop making those same mistakes. Of course there may be others that come up but God has already chosen you in spite of them and He will help you through those too.

No matter what people say about you or think about you it is all irrelevant. People may not understand you. In fact, they may not even like you. The only person we will give an account to is God Himself and we cannot blame others for decisions that we make.

Aren't you tired of failing? Aren't you tired of feeling like you don't belong here?

Walking in obedience is not the easiest thing in the world but I promise you it is the most fulfilling. I once heard a man of God say, it's "Thrills, Romance and Adventure". I have found that to be true!

As you put this book down I believe the power of God is going to challenge you and lift you no matter what situation you're in and no matter how many times you have failed. I believe the Holy Spirit is going to be wakening a desire within you to want to please Him and you are going to start sensing Him more and more in your life.

The key to keeping Him close to you is being obedient to Him. You cannot continually and intentionally keep disobeying Him and expect Him to reign in your life. It does not happen that way.

I pray that this book is an encouragement to you. I pray that you are challenged more than ever to live for Him because there are souls waiting on you. There are those around you that need you and the only way you will see them is if you are obedient and surrendered to Him who will tell you.

The thing you must remember is there are people that only you can reach. There are people that only I can reach. Will you walk in obedience and surrender to Jesus right now?

WALKING IN OBEDIENCE. It's the only way to live.